SUBDUING DEMONS IN AMERICA

SUBDUING DEMONS IN AMERICA

SELECTED POEMS 1962–2007

JOHN GIORNO

EDITED BY MARCUS BOON

SOFT SKULL
NEW YORK

Library of Congress Cataloging-in-Publication Data

Giorno, John.
Subduing demons in America : selected poems, 1962-2007 / John Giorno ; edited by Marcus Boon.
p. cm.
ISBN-13: 978-1-59376-204-9
ISBN-10: 1-59376-204-6
I. Boon, Marcus. II. Title.

PS3557.I53S83 2008
811'.54—dc22

2008014084

Cover design by Brett Yasko
Interior design by Pauline Neuwirth, Neuwirth & Associates, Inc.

Printed in the United States of America

Soft Skull Press
New York, NY

www.softskull.com

10 9 8 7 6 5 4 3 2 1

CONTENTS

Introduction ix

from *The American Book of the Dead,* 1964

Manifesto 1

Outlaw 2

Untitled Sequence 3

from *We Mean Business,* 1965

Subway 13

She Tasted Death 22

I'm Tired of Being Scared 24

The Marines Who Protested 25

from *Constitution of the United States,* 1966

Preamble 26

Article I, Sections 1 and 2 28

Article IV, Sections 2 and 4 43

Article VII 55

Notes 59

Poems, 1964–1969

Pornographic Poem 63

Capsule 66

Freaked 74

Head 80
Give It to Me, Baby 84
Flavor Grabber 94

John Giorno's Tarot Cards, 1968 100

from *Balling Buddha*, 1970
Johnny Guitar 108
Cunt 120
ESPE— 135
Electronic Sensory Poetry Environments
Poems, 1970
"I Looked the Soldier Guarding Me in the Eye" 139
"We Told Them to Bomb It" 140
She Half-Opened Her Eyes 141
"The Vietcong Take the Toads" 142
The Shouting Continued 143

from *Cancer in My Left Ball*, 1973
This Book is Cancer 144
Vajra Kisses 146
Dakini Software 157

from *Subduing Demons in America*, 1974
Suicide Sutra 185
from Subduing Demons in America 200

from *Shit Piss Blood Pus and Brains*, 1977 225

Poems 1975–1979
Eating the Sky 237
from Put Your Ear to Stone Open Your Heart to Sky 265
Grasping at Emptiness 276

from *You Got to Burn to Shine*, 1994

Life Is a Killer 296

I Resigned Myself to Being Here 302

Stretching It Wider 323

Exiled in Domestic Life 333

It's a Mistake to Think You're Special 338

Berlin & Chernobyl 343

Hi Risque 345

from *Everyone Gets Lighter*, 2007

Just Say No to Family Values 348

Everyone Gets Lighter 352

Down Comes the Rain 354

There Was a Bad Tree 360

La Saggezza Delle Streghe (Wisdom of the Witches) 368

Demons in the Details 372

Welcoming the Flowers 377

Thanx 4 Nothing 382

Acknowledgments 387

INTRODUCTION

by Marcus Boon

"Poetry's basic nature is Mind.
After it arises in the mind it can take countless forms."
—JOHN GIORNO

FOR MORE THAN forty years, poetry has poured forth from John Giorno in countless forms, from traditional lyric poems to epic sixty-plus-page double-column psychedelic pieces; from explosive visual and concrete silk-screened "poem-prints" to multitracked time-lagged audio poems performed in multisensory installations and happening spaces to explosive declamatory performances both solo and with a band in venues around the world; from LPs, CDs, and Dial-A-Poem poetry over the phone to fortune cookies, tarot cards, and more. The sheer variety of forms in which Giorno's poetry has manifested has won him fame and respect in places where to this day poetry hardly ever ventures, but has also resulted in a sometimes delightful, sometimes depressing confusion as to what exactly it is that John Giorno does. Is he really a poet? Is he an artist? A multimedia wizard? A Beat? A Buddhist? A rock 'n' roller? A Warholian Superstar?

Subduing Demons in America collects for the first time poems from throughout Giorno's career and gives an overview of Giorno's work, showing the true poet's heart that beats throughout all its many manifestations. Slipping through the cracks between genres and critical labels, many of the most extraordinary pieces in this book are appearing in print for the first time—even though they were often conceived of and initially developed as text on page. In the age of sampling, cut and paste, digital manipulation of text, appropriation as art form—which finds its peak in hip-hop and the textual orgy of the World Wide Web—the world is finally catching up with techniques and styles that Giorno pioneered several decades ago.

John Giorno was born on December 4, 1936, and grew up on Long Island, New York, in an Italian American family. He began writing poetry when he was fourteen ("very bad poetry!"), went to Columbia University as an undergraduate, and was quickly drawn into the enormously rich downtown New York cultural scene. His work took a decisive step when he met Andy Warhol, later becoming the star of Warhol's early film *Sleep*. Giorno recalls that "in the early 1960s, by chance a lot of my friends were artists—Andy Warhol, Bob Rauschenberg, Jasper Johns: the Pop artists. It's easy for me to say these names today, but in 1961 none of them were famous. It was 1961 was before Andy had a show, and Bob and Jasper, two years before, were very poor artists who barely had money for dinner. I saw them every other day, and saw how they worked with found images, what they did and what they didn't do, and intuitively understood why. Andy Warhol and I were lovers and so I would see in the late afternoon what he'd done that day. And it took a year and a half for me to say, "If they can do that with found images, why can't I do that in a similar way that has a similar impact using words?"

As a result, Giorno started working with appropriated texts from newspapers, making the found poems that form a part of *The American Book of the Dead* (written in 1964, excerpted in 1967's *Poems* but never published in full). The use of found material in poetry was nothing new, scriptural quotation having a long history in poetry, Pound and Eliot both cutting and pasting a variety of sources into "The Wasteland" and *The Cantos,* and Dos Passos famously sampling newspaper texts in *USA*. But just as the Pop artists used found images not as material for a montage or elements of some greater work, but as valid aesthetic objects in themselves, so Giorno presented his appropriations not as quotes, but as poems in their own right. However, if the Pop artists used the manipulation of color, scale, quantity, and quality of copies of the image as ways of turning an act of repetition into a generator of amazing novelty, Giorno of course had to draw upon other qualities of the written word. Still, rather than seeing his sources as "text," Giorno committed himself to particular images: "The images happened to be in word form: when my mind lit up, I collected them and then used them in making a poem. The only thing I was interested in was keeping the power of whatever it was I saw in a newspaper that made my attention sparkle. And the way I thought I could do this was through line breaks, which for me have to do with feeling. The feeling shifts with the line break."

The title *American Book of the Dead* is an appropriation from a Tibetan Buddhist burial manual, translated into English in 1927 by W. Y. Evans-Wentz as *The Tibetan Book of the Dead* and made newly popular by Timothy Leary in the early 1960s as the basis for an LSD trip manual. Another reference point is Warhol's disaster paintings of the early 1960s, themselves blown-up silk-screened appropriations from newspapers. The poems recontextualize familiar words (for example, a section of the Rolling Stones' anthem for samsara, "Satisfaction"), presenting them as a sequence, a serial montage of text images, a revealing pileup of American media debris similar to a gallery of Pop art.

While the Pop artists loved Giorno's work, his reception in the poetry world was decidedly mixed. Although Allen Ginsberg was a friend (and certainly none of Giorno's work could exist without the total freedom of content that "Howl" made possible), the form of these found poems was radically different from the mostly traditional lyrical stance of the Beats, and Ginsberg had little interest in his work. Similarly, although his poems shared an interest in the everyday as poetic object, Giorno's interest in appropriation and his connections to the Pop artists limited his relationship to New York School poets such as Frank O'Hara, who considered Warhol's work mere commercial painting without artistic merit. It was second-generation New York School poets such as Ted Berrigan who enjoyed Giorno's work, publishing him in his influential underground bible *C Magazine*. Giorno gave his first reading in a union building on 14th Street in February 1963 when Berrigan, after performing, said to Giorno, "Read your poems." "I was terrified!" Giorno recalls, at the same time quickly learning to savor the do-or-die energy of live performance.

Another inspiration for Giorno's 1960s work was the cut-up experiments that William S. Burroughs and Brion Gysin were undertaking at that time, literally slicing through text and reconfiguring it, setting discontinuous texts side by side in order to break through the control structures of grammar and rationality, revealing a turbulent linguistic chaos at once creative and destructive. Giorno met Burroughs and Gysin when they returned to New York from Paris in November 1964, and spent considerable time with them in 1965, when they were working on the manuscript for their cut-up manifesto *The Third Mind*. Giorno conducted some experiments with cut-ups, but never made it a formal part of his poetry, except insofar as cut-ups are a kind of montage. Gysin and Giorno became lovers, and Gysin introduced him to sound poetry and the use of the tape recorder as a tool for montaging and looping sounds and phrases. Gysin's own pioneering works of the period, such as the permutation poem "I Am What I Am," could be found in the French Domaine Poétique group's seminal "sound journal" *Revue OU*, which appeared on vinyl in the 1960s. Gysin and Giorno collaborated on a piece called "Subway Sound," recording sounds on the subway and manipulating them on twin reel-to-reel recorders. Gysin suggested that Giorno send the tape to Bernard Heidsieck, one of the main forces in the Parisian sound poetry scene, and the piece was played at the Paris Museum of Modern Art's Biennale in 1965—the start of Giorno's long and continuing participation in the European sound poetry scene, where he remains an influential and celebrated figure to this day.

Meeting Burroughs and Gysin politically radicalized Giorno. Cut-ups, for Burroughs especially, were not merely an aesthetic strategy but a way of breaking down a control system that operated through images and words, prescribing what could or could not be thought, and thus, what reality itself is. To quote one of Burroughs's favorite slogans, "Nothing is true, everything is permitted." Giorno's work slowly mutated from the formal considerations of many of the *Book of the Dead* poems, as well as works like his adaptation of an ornithological field guide, *Birds,* toward more overtly political poems, such as "The Constitution of the United States," written in 1966 during a six-month visit to Morocco. A work on the scale of Whitman's "Song of Myself" or Ginsberg's "Howl"—replacing their exuberant "I"s with a mostly third-person montage—the poem is at once an appropriation of the founding political document of the United States and a dissection, i.e., "cut-up," of the American media, revealing what America is constituted of. "Pornographic Poem," appropriated from a gay porn magazine in 1964, is an in-your-face celebration of gay male eroticism, written at a time when Burroughs was still on trial for obscenity in Massachusetts, and Stonewall and gay liberation were still years away—a powerful example of the way the act of labeling an otherwise highly marginal text "poetry," reshaping it through line and breath, affirming its value through signature, can unleash revolutionary poetic and political energies.

New York in the mid-1960s was in the middle of a major cultural renaissance, in which experimental electronic music, Pop art, dance, and performance came together in a profusion of happenings, installations, and multimedia events unfolding at venues such as New York's Judson Theater. Poetry was curiously and conspicuously absent in all of this. "There was almost never any sound system," Giorno recalls of reading in the early 1960s. "Poets actually just performed in St. Mark's Church with no microphone and nobody could hear anything but the echo. In 1963, Andy Warhol and I went to a reading at the Jill Kornblee Gallery—Frank O'Hara and John Ashbery. John had just moved back from Paris, and it was packed, and it was a hot May day. So they read their poetry and nobody could hear them. I would say, "I know there's sound there, but I can't hear!" and Andy would say, "It's so boring, why is it so boring?" It sounded like a drone, you couldn't hear a word. No one had even thought of having a microphone!"

In 1966, through his then-lover Robert Rauschenberg, who was at that time involved in a series of multimedia events called Experiments in Art and Technology (EAT) at the New York Armory, Giorno was introduced to synthesizer inventor Bob Moog. Giorno began visiting Moog at his factory in Trumansburg, in New York State, in 1967, and worked with Moog on synthesized treatments of his poems, presenting them as installations, or "ESPE—Electronic Sensory Poetry Environments," in a variety of public spaces including St. Mark's Church, the American Federation of Arts building, and the Central Park Bandshell. Conceived as multisensory pieces that are contemporaneous with Andy Warhol's Exploding Plastic Inevitable or Ken Kesey's West Coast Acid Tests, events out of which the modern rock 'n' roll show, the rave, and the disco evolved, Giorno's sound pieces pushed poetry firmly into the world of the psychedelic counterculture that was mushrooming around the world. A *New York Times* review of a Central Park performance in 1968 carried the nervous headline, "Outdoor Poetry Assaults Sense: Electronics and Strawberry Incense Turned On." A note at the back of 1970's *Balling Buddha* offers a more full inventory of effects, recording that when the poems "Johnny Guitar" and "Cunt" were played—using a "stereo Moog tape," six stereo speakers, and 4500 watts of multicolored lighting at St. Mark's in 1969—"a pitcher of LSD punch was on a table at the side of the altar. The audience was invited to help themselves. Each cup contained one-fourth of a trip. Five gallons of punch were given away."[1] Struggling to define what exactly was going on, the British underground magazine *Ginger Snaps* described Giorno as a "strobe poet, information s(p)licer."[2]

Giorno formed a not-for-profit production company, Giorno Poetry Systems, in 1965, which became the hub of an ever-proliferating series of multimedia manifestations of poetry, which to date includes 40 LPs and CDs, videos, films, and more. Giorno also

---

1 John Giorno, *Balling Buddha* (New York: Kulchur, 1970), 171.

2 *Ginger Snaps* (1972), (Kontexts, Exeter, UK), n.p.

organized the Dial-A-Poem series, beginning at the Architectural League of New York in 1967, making short poems by a broad range of contemporary poets, from Sylvia Plath to Taylor Mead, available over phone lines. The piece was repeated in 1970 at the Museum of Modern Art's "information" show and received millions of calls—conferring on Giorno superstar status while again amplifying the confusion as to whether he was part of the art, or poetry, or, for that matter, sound and music world.

Giorno's late-1960s poems see him expanding the use of found materials, including pornographic and countercultural texts, as well as the use of repetition. Indeed, poems like "Capsule," "Give It to Me, Baby," and "Johnny Guitar" are among the most rock 'n' roll poems ever written, every bit as psychedelic and confrontational as The Stooges or Jefferson Airplane, and probably just as much the product of a wide-ranging armory of pharmaceuticals, which, as Giorno has repeatedly insisted, have the potential to open and expand the mind and bring bliss. *Balling Buddha,* a multicolor confection printed on pages in the six colors of the rainbow, rather than traditional black on white, introduced Giorno's signature split lines running down the center of each page—as a way of both reproducing the multitracking used in his sound poems and perturbing the linear flow of text on the page. Giorno observes that the split line "breaks the lineal flow. Because you're no longer just reading left to right and down. And then the repetitions have to do with slowing the mind because when you read something twice you perceive it in a different way because your mind sees it in a different way. In performance those devices work in a more musical way: Repetitions are like songs—a song is a repetition, and the second repeating of a line changes its tonal qualities. When I repeat a line in performance, very intentionally every repetition is said from a different point of view. And in rehearsing a poem, the musical qualities inherent in the words and phrases are discovered and developed, and become fixed as a song."

Other points of reference for the dual columns include Warhol's split-screen cine-epic *Chelsea Girls* and the Velvet Underground's spooky dual monologue "The Murder Mystery," both of which push narrative discontinuity to a limit through simultaneous double streams of data. Poems like "Johnny Guitar" have developed far beyond "appropriation" to encompass a wide range of ways of making a poetic montage, breaking apart found materials and placing them alongside apparently unrelated materials—yet as with the Warhol and Velvet Underground pieces, not abandoning narrative altogether. Like Warhol, and to the chagrin of proponents of the avant-garde such as Richard Kostelanetz, who claimed that Giorno's work is built on "all the traditional baggage,"[3] Giorno has remained continuously committed to the notion that conventional everyday syntax and imagery conceals within it powerfully transcendent and, for that matter, "abstract" energies, which wait to be revealed through inspired acts of reconfiguration.

Balling Buddha features some of Giorno's earliest explorations of Asian religious texts and images. Giorno was first introduced to Buddhism as an undergraduate at Columbia, where, from 1956 to 1958, he took classes in the newly established "Oriental Civilization" program created by William Theodore de Bary. The program offered almost no study of Tibetan Buddhism, since very little was known about Tibet. It was only with the 1959 takeover of Tibet by China, and the ensuing flight to India of many of the great lamas (and ordinary citizens) facing persecution and probable death at the hands of the Chinese, that Tibetan Buddhism became accessible to Westerners. In the 1960s, Tibetan settlements sprang up throughout the Indian Himalaya, and a small stream of Westerners, including the poets Allen Ginsberg, Gary Snyder, and Joanne Kyger, visited them. However, very few Tibetan teachers visited America in the 1960s; Chögyam Trungpa Rinpoche, the lama most associated with spreading Tibetan Buddhism in North America, did not visit until 1970, and it was rare to find an American or European practicing Tibetan Buddhism.[4]

---

3 Richard Kostelanetz, *The Old Poetries and the New* (Ann Arbor: U. Michigan P., 1981), 193–5.

4 See Rick Fields, *How the Swans Came to the Lake: A Narrative History of Buddhism in America.* Third ed. (Boston: Shambhala, 1992), 273–338.

Although there were opportunities to practice Zen meditation in New York at that time, Giorno didn't take advantage of them. In a 1974 interview, he observed that his attitude had been "just the usual 1960s 'take LSD and see Buddha.'"[5] It was a visit with Allen Ginsberg that finally pushed Giorno toward practice, and in March 1971 he arrived in India. Traveling with friends, Giorno visited His Holiness the Dalai Lama and studied Tibetan religion and language before meeting His Holiness Dudjom Rinpoche, the supreme head of the Nyingma, one of the four main schools of Tibetan Buddhism, who was to become his guru. Dudjom Rinpoche is considered one of the great scholars of Tibetan Buddhism of the twentieth century, and a master meditator and yogi. He was also considered a great poet, writing down revealed teachings (or Terma) in poetic form. Giorno returned to India many times to study and live close to H. H. Dudjom Rinpoche in the 1970s, and in 1976 he invited him to America. Giorno also studied with many of the other great living Nyingma lamas, including Dilgo Khyentse Rinpoche, Kangyur Rinpoche, and Chatral Rinpoche. He was also one of the first students to study with Chögyam Trungpa Rinpoche when he arrived in America, and in the early 1970s did many retreats at Tail of the Tiger at Karmê Chöling, the retreat center that Trungpa established in Vermont.

Giorno is emphatic that he does not regard himself as a "Buddhist poet," seeing Buddhism and poetry as separate parts of his life. Nevertheless, *Cancer in My Left Ball,* published by Dick Higgins's Something Else Press in 1972, represents a leap forward in the quality of Giorno's work, one that it's difficult not to attribute in part to his exposure to living Buddhist teachers. Many of the elements in the poems, including the use of found texts, the split/double line running down the page, the use of repetition, and the juxtaposition of sacred, pornographic, and political materials are the same as those found in *Poems* and *Balling Buddha.* But the arbitrary juxtaposition of stanzas in the earlier poems, reminiscent

5 Winston Leyland, "Winston Leyland Interview: John Giorno," *Gay Sunshine Interviews, Vol. 1*, ed. Winston Leyland, 130–162 (San Francisco: Gay Sunshine Press, 1978), 132.

of Burroughs and Gysin's cut-ups, has been replaced by chaotic, pulsating fluxes of phrases which no longer read like a formal experiment in collage, or an attempt to replicate certain delay effects made possible by the use of tapes in Giorno's late-1960s sound environments. Instead, they have the quality of a meditating mind, a mind observing itself and its environment and trying to provide a representation in words of what it sees and hears, using all the available strategies of the twentieth-century avant-garde.

When Giorno says of his poetry that it is words, lines that arise in the mind (either his or those he finds around him) that he works with in different ways, he is framing things in a manner that is different from traditional lyrical approaches, in which words are considered a true reflection of self, but different also from the avant-garde tradition, which posits that there is no such thing as a self and therefore only random, indeterminate aggregations of meaning exist. Giorno's poetry suggests thought as it appears to a meditator who has been instructed neither to grasp nor hold on to particular thoughts, nor to push thoughts away or repress them, but rather to let thoughts arise in the mind in a natural way, coming and going, arising into awareness without attraction or aversion. The words thus are neither his, nor *not* his. In these poems, Giorno becomes a *bricoleur* of his own thoughts—as every poet is.

Perhaps this is the place for some advice on how to read a John Giorno poem: However you like, of course; or, to quote Giorno's advice to me on editing this book, "See how it arises in your mind." Giorno, for me, is a poet whose work sometimes actually benefits from being skimmed or scanned, and in reading him, it helps to tune in to a tempo (as indeed one does with anything one reads, though habit allows us to ignore this), and let the words flow over you, almost like a meditator becoming silently aware of the coming and going of thoughts in his or her mind. Walter Benjamin spoke of the revolutionary qualities of distraction, manifesting as a kind of dreamy repetition that dissolves the self and allows powerful insight to emerge seemingly out of nowhere. Giorno, as both our foremost portrayer of sleep in the movies and a self-confessed connoisseur of sleep of many kinds, works with this energy, and readers should avail themselves of it too, without a feeling of duty or obligation to conventional ways of reading or the apparent order of words on the page, however elegant and refined they unquestionably are. Giorno exposes the discontinuities that are an essential part of our reading and writing practices, offering the reader a genuinely psychedelic experience of encounter with text—and with one's own mind. Poems like "Subduing Demons in America" offer some of the most phenomenologically accurate renderings of what thinking actually is ever to be written down.

Having said that, Giorno's poems from the 1970s also give us a powerfully intimate portrait of the life of a gay man in post-Stonewall New York City, complete with descriptions of cruising the downtown streets, bathhouses, anonymous sex in public lavatories, and discotheques. With his use of cut-up quotes from disco songs, his fascination with effects of echo and repetition, and his celebration of pleasure and heartbreak, Giorno's poetry runs strangely parallel to the sonic magicians of the five boroughs, such as Grandmaster Flash or Larry Levan, who were discovering, via the same potent brew of NYC sonic overload and an arsenal of mind-altering chemicals, the mixing and editing techniques that would bring the world the twelve-inch disco-mix single, the sampling and mixing of hip-hop, and the sonic hall of mirrors of techno. They also contain records of Giorno's studies with Tibetan Buddhist masters—notably H. H. Dudjom Rinpoche—both in the form of quotes from his teachers and fragmentary reflections on the ups and downs of his own practice. To the confusion of defenders of the classical avant-garde, Giorno uses montage and other "experimental" techniques, but is in fact a realist, not in the sense of following that jumble of nineteenth-century cultural conventions usually associated with the word, but in terms of telling things how they are.

In the 1970s, Giorno deepened his association with William Burroughs, who returned to America from Europe in 1974 and moved into The Bunker, the locker room of the former YMCA on the Bowery in Manhattan, where Giorno has lived since the

1960s. While continuing to issue an ever more remarkable set of LP recordings of Burroughs and other writers and poets on Giorno Poetry Systems, Giorno toured with Burroughs, developing an increasingly powerful live performance style, which at some points threatened to eclipse his interest in text-based poems. Nevertheless, all of the poems that Giorno performed live and on audio recordings began as text-based poems, and his performances, however spontaneous and outrageous, are generally accurate renditions of written texts, worked and reworked over months and years through oral performance.

Giorno's work increasingly found an audience and a context in the burgeoning new wave and punk scenes, whose participants could relate to the fierce, wrathful energy that manifests in classic 1970s poems like "Grasping at Emptiness" or "Suicide Sutra." Giorno released the work of Laurie Anderson; performed alongside Patti Smith at the key 1978 celebration of William Burroughs, the Nova Convention; released music by Sonic Youth, Karen Finley, Lydia Lunch, and others on Giorno Poetry Systems; and formed his own new wave rock band, the John Giorno Band, who performed around the United States in the 1980s. Giorno's experiments with sound poetry have been cited as a major influence by industrial music pioneers Throbbing Gristle's Genesis P-Orridge, and Giorno has remained in contact with T. G. offshoots such as Coil. Electro-punk pioneers Suicide's 1975 masterpiece "Frankie Teardrop," with its graphic portrayal of urban decay, sounds remarkably like a dynamic reworking of Giorno's 1973 classic "Suicide Sutra." This poem—amazingly, Giorno's first poem not based on found material—"received enormous radio play across America and Europe for many years," recalls Giorno. "Many stories got back to me about the effect of the poem. One young man in San Francisco was attempting suicide when he heard it on the radio, and the next day called the station to say 'You saved my life.'"

Giorno's use of transgressive, provocative, or pornographic materials, which links him superficially to the punk and no wave scenes, lacks the nihilistic worldview that much of these scenes remains trapped in. Although conservatives might think of Giorno's work as transgressive or shocking, informed by or experienced through a Buddhist meditation practice, all thoughts that arise in the mind are in a sense free of labels, including the most obscene and the most mundane ones. Indeed there are Tibetan Buddhist meditation practices, such as Chöd, in which a meditator deliberately focuses on the most supposedly or conventionally horrific images, precisely to see that they are illusory mental constructs and nothing to be afraid of—or attached to. Giorno observes that "I was a gay man living in this world at the end of the twentieth century. What I did in my everyday life was what everyone else did. So if it seems like rough S & M images, difficult images, it's what the world is made of. I wasn't trying to create something that was other than what it is. So all those images were just the world around me. And the point of it all was that these images are just as empty as anything, or everything, miraculously appearing, their empty nature is the empty nature of all phenomena."

To use these images in the poem as found material was then to liberate them from conventional meanings, from homophobic fear or commodified desire, and from the ignorance that makes us believe in the inherent reality of all phenomena, as the Buddha taught in the second of the four noble truths. To quote Giorno from one of the remarkably candid interviews he did with *Gay Sunshine* magazine: "Compassion for gay men and gay women has been the object of my life's work. Even before I knew what I was doing, I was doing it. Before I knew that what was arising in my heart was called compassion. Those early 1960s poems that were pornographic, in your face, were intended to break all concepts. I wanted to liberate myself and the poem, so that everyone would be free."[6]

Despite, or perhaps because of the abundant hedonism that characterizes Giorno's poems from the 1970s, there is a growing sense of fatigue, even despair in late-1970s works such as "Eating

6 Leyland, op cit, 275.

the Sky" and "Grasping at Emptiness." AIDS and Ronald Reagan struck America around 1980, decimating the arts community through disease, funding cuts, and a "return" to a Christian morality bankrolled by covert arms sales and other scandals. Giorno's response was twofold. In 1984 he started an AIDS charity, the AIDS Treatment Project, and devoted considerable amounts of his time and energy to helping people with AIDS. In his poetry, Giorno gave up use of found material in 1981, working instead with words as they came into his mind. His poems from the 1980s have the pared-down, amped-up force of early rappers such as Run-DMC, honed in performance with William S. Burroughs and with his own rock band, with whom he performed for seven years. Giorno was a pioneer of the use of amplified visual and textual slogan-poems, as later popularized by artists like Jenny Holzer and Barbara Kruger—an aggressive, focused counter-propaganda to the ads and infotainment cranked out by the Christian right and Republicans, intoxicated, even aroused by the very concerns and activities they claimed to want to banish. The slogan poems were also a powerful influence on the punk and hardcore scenes—Black Flag's riotous badmouthing and Henry Rollins's spoken-word career come to mind, not to mention the psychedelic nihilism of bands like Flipper and the Butthole Surfers. Giorno's work has continued to resonate with many of the most interesting and innovative younger poets: the Nuyorican and slam poetry scenes, the media poem interventions of Bob Holman, Edwin Torres's startling sound pieces, Kenneth Goldsmith's all-devouring media appropriations, and the hip-hop dada experiments of Harryette Mullen.

Of his more recent poems, Giorno says: "They are more like songs. Since I took the path of breaking with Modernism and traditional poetic forms, I have had no one to teach me, and had to invent it all myself, with no help. The early years of experimenting, I think of as walking blindfolded through traffic, and not getting killed. It has been one continuous ever-changing development from 1962 to 2007."

Giorno's ability to move between different registers, from Dzogchen meditation to the raw turbulence of everyday human emotions, has grown over the years, both on the page and in his live performances, which continue to tear the house down whether he's performing at the St. Mark's Poetry Project New Year's reading or in festivals in Europe, where his work has been celebrated and published in a way that has yet to happen in America.

A note of gentleness, sweetness even, can be heard in the poems from his most recent collection, *Everyone Gets Lighter,* reflecting a hard-won wisdom, compassion, and strength—an ability to bear tough situations and transform them sometimes. The Buddhist perspective in "Welcoming the Flowers" or "The Bad Tree" never feels forced, and it is not necessary to have any particular knowledge to engage fully with the poems, which resonate directly with the reader or listener's everyday experience. There is a self in these poems, but Giorno registers its flickering, surging, and disappearing quality with humor and sadness, leading one to think that perhaps as he's grown older, John Giorno has subdued some of his own demons.

All otherwise unattributed quotes from Giorno are taken from an interview with the author, conducted in New York City, March 10, 2005.

SUBDUING DEMONS IN AMERICA

MANIFESTO

We hold
these truths
to be self-evident,
that all men
are created equal,
that they are endowed
by their Creator
with certain unalienable rights,
that among these are
Life,
Liberty
and the pursuit of happiness.

John Giorno
(1964)

OUTLAW

A bearded outlaw
who claimed
he was an immortal
descendent
of God
was killed
last night
by the police.

(1963)

UNTITLED SEQUENCE

A harness racing horse
panicked aboard an airliner
8,000 feet above the Pacific yesterday
and almost leaped into the cockpit
before the flight engineer killed him
with a fire ax.

Cops in Pulaski, Tenn.,
load Rudolph Luik, 25,
into ambulance
after he was picked up
for speeding.
When police
began to tail him,
he took off clothes.
It took six men
to strap him
to stretcher.

A plainclothesman
was beaten to his knees
by a mob of teen-age girls yesterday
when he and his partner
tried to break up a fight
between two girl gangs
in a schoolyard
in the Bedford-Stuyvesant section
of Brooklyn.

Leslie Douglas Ashley,
a female impersonator
and one of the Federal Bureau
of Investigation's
10 most wanted criminals,
was arrested today
while working
at a carnival.
He had escaped
from a Texas mental hospital
while awaiting trial
on murder charges.

I can't get no
satisfaction
I can't get no
satisfaction
cause I try
and I try
and I try
and I try
I can't get no
I can't get no
no no no
that's what I say
I can't get no
I can't get no
I can't get no
satisfaction
no satisfaction
no satisfaction
no satisfaction

DIRECTIONS:
Shake
before using.
Remove
protective plastic cap.
Hold spout
next to palm of hand
and release
puff of foam
about size of quarter.
Rub hands together;
spread lightly
over skin,
stockings
and other thin clothing,
reapplying as needed
to cover
all exposed areas.

DIRECTIONS:
Hold can
2 or 3 inches
from surface.
Press button
on top of can.
Spray
only until area
is wetted.
This will dry quickly
to a water-washable
nonstaining film.
May be repeated
as necessary
for minor burns,
non-venomous
insect bites
and poison ivy.

Slowly,
with his 13-month-old son
in his arms,
the man walked out
of the silent apartment
at 544 E. 11th St.,
near Avenue B,
shortly after
7 AM yesterday.
There was
a street phone booth
nearby,
and he dialed
the Communications Bureau
at Police Headquarters.

"I've just killed my wife!"
he blurted.

Astronaut Jim Lovell,
flying in Gemini 7
high over Hawaii,
today spotted
a tiny pinpoint
of greenish-blue brilliance
far below.
He successfully "locked on"
for 40 seconds
and sent
the world's first communication
down a laser beam
to earth.

"I've got it," Lovell cried.

A 56-year-old
Forest Hills woman
was stabbed four times
and critically wounded
by a stickup man yesterday
in Maple Grove Cemetery,
Kew Gardens, Queens,
as she was visiting
her husband's grave.

(1962–64)

SUBWAY

Downtown
To Express Trains Only
To Uptown Local
Use Stairs
At Either End
Of This Platform

1 AQUARIUM

IND
BMT W 8 ST

2 AQUEDUCT RACE TRACK

IRT AQUEDUCT

Big Bold Beautiful—Big "A"

3 BROOKLYN BOTANIC GARDEN

IRT EASTERN PARKWAY
BMT BOTANIC GARDEN

Preparation H
shrinks
hemorrhoids
without surgery
Stops itch
Relieves pain

Does she

or doesn't she?
Hair color
so natural
only her hairdresser
knows for sure

4 CARNEGIE HALL

BMT 57 ST
IRT
IND 59 ST

Music
in the air
everywhere

Be a hairstylist
in 6 ½ months

12 free
outdoor
concerts
by 106 man
New York Philharmonic

Licensed
by the State
of New York

5 CHINATOWN

IRT
BMT CANAL ST

Worlds Fair Trains
Use Uptown Trains
To Times Square
Change
For Flushing Trains

6 THE CLOISTERS

7 COLISEUM

Girl, 12, Slays
A Stranger On
IND Platform

8 CONEY ISLAND

IND
BMT CONEY ISLAND

9 EMPIRE STATE BUILDING

Award Winning
Ingerid School
Of Hair Design

Are You
In The Psoriasis
Shadow?
Scales
Redness
Itch…
Respond
To Psorex
For Temporary Relief
In Many Cases

Sleep cool tonight
$119.95

To the moon
and beyond
beyond
beyond
beyond
beyond
beyond

Touch:
The communicator of love

Population explosion

Call Ju 2 3222

10 FREEDOMLAND

Free trial session

A doctor
tells you

why touch
is so important
to wives
to husbands
to children
Read why
it can communicate
when words
are useless
And how foolish
we are
not to make use
of this the greatest cure
for loneliness
there is
In August
Reader's
Digest

Headache?
Take Aspirin
Tension?
Take Compoz

Sobol told
the cops
the girl approached
the woman and
from a distance
of six feet
hurled
a hunting knife
with a six inch blade
The knife struck
the woman flatly

and clattered harmlessly
on the platform
"do you know me?"
The startled woman
asked her assailant
Without a word
the girl walked over
calmly picked up
the knife
and plunged it twice
into the woman's chest

11 GRANT'S TOMB

IRT 125 ST

12 GUGGENHEIM MUSEUM

IRT 86 ST LEX AVE

13 J.F. KENNEDY INT'L AIRPORT

You don't have
to be Jewish
to love Levy's
real Jewish rye

Mount Sinai Hospital
96th Street

14 JEWISH MUSEUM

IRT 96 ST LEX AVE

Notice
All Persons
Are Forbidden
To Enter Upon
Or Cross
The Tracks
Interborough
Rapid Transit Co

15 LAGUARDIA AIRPORT

16 MUSEUM OF NATURAL HISTORY

IND 81 ST
IRT 79 ST

17 NEW YORK HISTORICAL SOCIETY

IND 81 ST
IRT 79 ST

Spitting
On the Platform
Or Other Parts
Of This Station
Is UNLAWFUL
Offenders
Are Liable
To Arrest
By Order
Of the Board
Of Health

Save Water
Now

***from* WE MEAN BUSINESS, 1965**

18 NEW YORK STOCK EXCHANGE

You can help
a diabetic boy
or girl

19 POLO GROUNDS

For temporary relief
from simple nervous
tension

20 ROCKEFELLER CENTER

21 ROCKAWAY BEACH

every summer
Camp NYDA
offers 350 diabetic
boys and girls
a month's vacation
They learn to cope
with their diabetes
while having the fun
of camp life
Helping these children
will give you
real satisfaction

For Real Satisfaction
Smoke Camels
The Real Cigarette

Satisfy

your smoking taste
with Madison
little cigars
even without
inhaling

22 ST. PATRICKS CATHEDRAL

23 STATUE OF LIBERTY

24 TEMPLE EMANU-EL

25 TRINITY CHURCH

26 UNITED NATIONS

Follow Blue Arrow

Send your gift to

reconstituted
lemon juice

The Destroyers

104 East 40th Street
New York 16, N. Y.

(1965)

Bob Friede
was 25 years old,
barely five feet
eight inches tall,
and weighed
no more than
135 pounds.
His light-brown hair
was uncombed,
and the pupils
of his blue eyes
were "pinned",
constricted
from a shot
of heroin
he had pumped
into himself.
He wore
dirty black dungarees
and a dirty shirt.
He did not look
at all like
a graduate
of Dartmouth
or like a member
of a rich philanthropic
publishing family
or like the beneficiary
of a trust fund
that gave him
an allowance
of $27,000 a year.

She came
from the suburbs
intelligent
and attractive,
and troubled,
from a comfortable home
and a proud family,
and for two years,
with increasing frequency,
she "turned on".
She tasted marijuana
and amphetamines
and LSD,
and then, one day
early this year,
at the age
of 19,
she tasted
death.

(1965)

from **WE MEAN BUSINESS, 1965**

I'M TIRED OF BEING SCARED

An unemployed
machinist,
who traveled
here
from Georgia
10 days ago,
and who could not
find a job,
walked into
a police station
yesterday
and said,
"I'm tired of being scared."

(1965)

THE MARINES WHO PROTESTED

The marines
who protested
the air base
in this area,
close to
North Vietnam,
appeared almost
unanimous today
in criticizing
the cease-fire.

The attitude
varied little
from privates
on the perimeter
to generals
in the rear.

“Either you fight
or you don’t fight,”
a company commander said.
“You don’t stop fighting
because it’s Dec. 25.”

(1965)

from WE MEAN BUSINESS, 1965

PREAMBLE

WE THE PEOPLE
of the United States,
in order to form
a more perfect Union,
establish Justice,
insure domestic Tranquility,
provide for the common defense,
promote the general Welfare,
and secure the Blessings of Liberty
to ourselves and our Posterity,
do ordain,
and establish
this CONSTITUTION
for the United States
of America.

The Liberty Bell Shrine
houses an exact replica
of the bell
within the original walls
which protected it
in 1777–78.

After two days
and three nights
of being lost
in the city's
subway system,
a 21-year-old

retarded youth
stumbled home
last night
to his anxious
family.

James Modesto
said he was "tired"
as he entered
the flat
at 183 Bainbridge Street
in the Bedford-Stuyvesant
section of Brooklyn.
Then he cried.

ARTICLE I

Section 1 All legislative Powers
herein granted
shall be vested
in a Congress
of the United States,
which shall consist
of a Senate
and a House of Representatives.

Members
of the New York
Police Department
and medical experts
will meet with municipal
and federal officials
in Brooklyn
on Friday
to consider ways
of curtailing
the increasing use
of LSD,
the hallucinatory
drug.

THIS IS
YOUR BOARDING PASS

Please
carry it
with you
when deplaning
at intermediate points.

Two passengers
were killed yesterday
when a violent Atlantic storm
pounded the Italian luxury liner
Michelangelo
as she headed for New York.

from **CONSTITUTION OF THE UNITED STATES, 1966**

ARTICLE I

Section 2 The House of Representatives
shall be composed of Members
chosen every second year
by the People
of the several States,
and the Electors
in each State
shall have the Qualifications
requisite for Electors
of the most numerous Branch
of the State Legislature.

A new way
to see the U.S.A.
without spending
too much time
or money.

The U.S. Air Force reported today
that the first B-52 raid
on North Vietnam
set off huge landslides
which sealed the strategic
Mu Gia Pass
through which the Communists
funnel men and supplies

to the Viet Cong
in South Vietnam.
The only legal
United States source
of LSD,
the controversial
mind-distorting drug,
has halted
distribution of it
in this country.

Twenty thousand Buddhist
demonstrators
marched in Saigon late today
in a "victory ceremony"
after the military government
issued a decree
promising elections
for a civilian government
in the next three
to five months.

Donald Dilworth Jr., 21,
was married April 3,
inducted at Fort Dix April 4,
died at Fort Dix April 11.

from **CONSTITUTION OF THE UNITED STATES, 1966**

Tiffany
folding ring
travel clock
that fits
into its own
leather case.
Eight-day,
fifteen-jewel
movement
with alarm,
$82.

Heavy buying
moved into today's
stock market
sending prices
up sharply in spots
and building up
to high volume
that put turnover
past 10 million shares
shortly after 2 o'clock.

No person
shall be a Representative
who shall not have attained
the age of twenty-five years,
and been seven years a Citizen

of the United States,
and who shall not,
when elected,
be an Inhabitant of that State
in which he shall be chosen.

Robert Friedo, 25,
received a suspended sentence today
on his plea of guilty
to second-degree manslaughter
in the narcotics-overdose death
of 19-year-old Celeste Crenshaw.

"We visited
our boy
his last day
in Fort Dix,"
said the father,
Donald Dilworth,
a construction engineer,
126 Hirshfeld Place,
New Milford, N.J.

"They told us
he had bronchitis.
He was gasping
for breath."

"We gave him water,
and the nurse said,
'Let him get the water

for himself,
it will be good
for him.'"

Representatives
and direct Taxes
shall be apportioned
among the several States
which may be included
within this Union,
according to their respective Numbers,
which shall be determined
by adding the whole Number
of free Persons,
including those bound to Service
for a Term of Years,
and excluding Indians not taxed,
three-fifths of all other Persons.
The actual Enumeration
shall be made within three Years
after the first Meeting
of the Congress
of the United States,
and within every subsequent Term
of ten Years,
in such a manner as they shall
by Law direct.
The Number of Representatives
shall not exceed
one for every thirty Thousand,
but each State shall have
at Least one Representative;
and until such enumeration

shall be made,
the State of New Hampshire
shall be entitled to choose three,
Massachusetts eight,
Rhode Island and Providence Plantations one,
Connecticut five,
New York six,
New Jersey four,
Pennsylvania eight,
Delaware one,
Maryland six,
Virginia ten,
North Carolina five,
South Carolina five,
and Georgia three.

Five-year-old
Donna Wingenroth
is home again
and doctors hope
she will suffer
no permanent
mental damage
from eating
a sugar cube
containing LSD.

United States officials said today
that for the first time
in the Vietnam war
more American servicemen

were killed
during a one-week
period of fighting
than South Vietnamese soldiers.

"Someone else told us
he had double pneumonia,
and they told us
he would walk out
of the hospital
the next day."
"They said
he was just tired,
but he was choking
to death."

"We asked for oxygen
but they said
the doctor didn't write
oxygen on his order."

America's first B-52 raid
against Communist North Vietnam
delivered a bomb load
of 1.4 million pounds
which sent whole mountainsides
crashing down onto the approaches
to the Ho Chi Minh Trail,
it was disclosed today.

“We begged
for oxygen
for our son
and three hours later
they sent up a tank.
No inhalator,
just a tube
to put in his nose.”

Air Force Officials called it
the greatest single bombing raid
since World War II,
far surpassing any raids
of the war in Korea
and probably the most destructive
since the atomic bomb
was dropped on Nagasaki
in August 1945.

When vacancies happen
in the Representation
from any State,
the Executive Authority
thereof shall issue
Writs of Election
to fill such Vacancies.

from **CONSTITUTION OF THE UNITED STATES, 1966**

The Defense Department
said today
South Vietnam's
civil disorders
have resulted
in a shortage of bombs
for the air war,
reducing bombing operations
against the Viet Cong.

Dr. Timothy Leary,
leading spokesman
for the mind-altering
drug LSD,
has urged
all his followers
to give up
the use
of the drug
as well as marijuana
for one year
while trying
to convert
their parents
and elders
to new forms
of mind expansion
without drugs.

Mrs. Jacqueline Kennedy
chats with Antonio Garrigues,

Spanish ambassador
to the Holy See,
while watching
the bullfights
in Seville.
She is wearing
the high comb and mantilla
characteristic of Andalusia.

"I asked
the nurse
if our son
was critical,
and she said,
'If he was critical
he would be
in the critical ward.
This is not
the critical ward.
He'll be out
tomorrow.
Come back
tomorrow
and he will
walk out
to see you.'"

A Harvard-educated
medical student
charged with murdering
his 57-year-old

mother-in-law
while “flying high”
on LSD,
was set free
by Bellevue Hospital’s
psychiatric division
after he was sent there
three weeks ago
under the spell
of the mind-bending drug,
The Journal-American
learned today.

Leave			Arrive
Man has set	Flush ing	Wood side	New York
AM	AM	AM	AM
12:07	12:27	12:34	12:43

The House of Representatives
shall choose their speaker
and other Officers;
and shall have the sole Power
of Impeachment.

"At 7:30
that night
the nurse
told us
to leave,
saying again
we should
come back
tomorrow
and see him
walk out
to say
hello."

"They called us
the next morning
at 6 o'clock
and said
our son
was dead."

Luna 10,
the Soviet vehicle
in orbit
around the moon,
has obtained
a gamma ray spectrum
of the lunar surface
indicating that the moon
has a crust

and that this crust
is somewhat
like the earth's.

"I went
to Fort Dix
and talked to them,
but it's like talking
to a stone wall."

ARTICLE IV

Section 2 The Citizens
of each State
shall be entitled
to all Privileges
and Immunities
of Citizens
in the several States.

This booklet
has been prepared
to assist you
in discharging
your duties
in an efficient
and intelligent
manner.
You are urged
to study it
carefully.

Euill Long, 58,
of 25 Market St., Newark,
interrupted his arraignment
on a homicide charge
before Bergen County
Superior Court Judge
Benjamin P. Galanti,
to cry out:

from **CONSTITUTION OF THE UNITED STATES, 1966**

"Don't bother.
I don't want to be tried.
I killed her.
I did it.
I did it."

Color television stocks
leaped as much as $8 higher
and featured in a strong and active
stock market today.

A huge orange fireball
and thick black smoke
curled from the swamps
after the eight-engine
Stratofortresses
unloaded their 750 pound bombs.
An Air Force spokesman said
a Communist jungle mine factory
hidden among mangroves 40 feet high
apparently had been obliterated.

He described
the strike
as "the most awesome
and devastating thing
I ever had seen."

Earlier,
while being questioned
in Harrison police station,

he was reported
to have volunteered:
"I know her from around
and knew her name.
I killed her
with a window sash,
a steel sash."

A Person
charged
in any State
with Treason,
Felony,
or other Crime,
who shall flee
from Justice,
and be found
in another State
shall, on Demand
of the executive Authority
of the State
from which he fled,
be delivered up,
to be removed
to the State
having Jurisdiction
of the Crime.

Motorola spurted
nearly a dozen points
before subsiding,
Zenith and Magnavox
also climbed
in the color TV
group.

I *can* write.

I *could* sing in those days.

He *could* sing if he tried.

If I *could* sing, I would.

"I'm guilty.
I plead no defense,"
said the suspect
Euill W. Long, 58,
at his arraignment
before Bergen County
Court Judge Benjamin Galanti
in Hackensack.

The party
who commences
the lawsuit
is called
the plaintiff.
In criminal cases
the State of New York
is always the plaintiff.

The party
against whom
the action
is brought
is called
the defendant.
A party
may be an individual
or may be a firm
or corporation.

MORE THAN A MOISTURIZER,
MORE THAN A LUBRICANT.

“Source of Beauty”
releases the beauty
imprisoned in a dry complexion
by supplementing
the natural oils and moisture
that age steals away.
Combining lavish lubricants
and super-moisturizers,
this high-potency formula
keeps your skin
looking fresh,
young and lovely.
Helps ease away
fine lines and puffiness,
encourages elasticity...
swings the pendulum of time
in a new, young direction.

25.00 and 15.00

from **CONSTITUTION OF THE UNITED STATES, 1966**

Ten hours
after a 15-year-old
Newark girl
was bludgeoned
to death,
her brother
today captured
a man who confessed
to the murder.

These delicious cookies
are made from:
flour,
sugar,
shortening,
oats,
invert sugar,
molasses,
raisins,
dairy whey,
salt,
bicarbonate of soda,
ammonium bicarbonate,
lecithin,
pure ground spices,
artificial flavors,
U.S. certified colors.

The Supreme Court
today backed up
the Justice Department's
use of federal law
in civil rights murders
that have gone unpunished
by local authorities.

No Person
held to Service
or Labor
in one State,
under the Laws thereof,
escaping into another,
shall, in Consequence
of any Law
or Regulation therein,
be discharged
from such Service
or Labor,
but shall be delivered up
to whom such Service
or Labor
may be due.

TO THE PERSON SUMMONED
IF YOU WISH TO PLEAD GUILTY,
YOU MAY PAY FIFTEEN (15) DOLLARS,
THE PRESCRIBED FINE
FOR THIS PARKING OFFENSE,
ON OR BEFORE

***from* CONSTITUTION OF THE UNITED STATES, 1966**

THE RETURN DATE
OF THE SUMMONS,
DIRECT BY MAIL
AND PAYABLE TO:

The brother,
Dennis Van Orden, 19,
said the man confessed
battering his sister, Penny,
over the head
with a lead pipe.

Your reward
in serving
as a juror
lies in the fact
that you have performed
a high duty
of citizenship
by aiding
in the maintenance
of law and order
and in the administration
of justice
among your fellow men.
It is hoped
that your contribution
to this important function
of government
will be an enlightening
and interesting experience
and that at the conclusion

of your service
you will enjoy
the satisfaction
of having performed
an important duty.

Popular Music
That Will Live
Forever

ARTICLE IV

Section 4 The United States
shall guarantee
to every State
in this Union
a Republican Form
of Government,
and shall protect
each of them
against Invasion;
and on Application
of the Legislature,
or of the Executive
(when the Legislature
can not be convened),
against domestic
Violence.

AVCO Corp.
Cincinnati, Ohio

Procurement
of additional equipment
for early warning systems

SEA launched
ballistic missile
warning system

$10,500,000

Four hooded gunmen,
using smoke bombs
to cover their retreat,
today robbed the jewelry section
of a fashionable department store
of an estimated $500,000
worth of diamonds,
sapphires, rubies, and emeralds.

THE SOFT MACHINE
by William S. Burroughs.
182 pages. Grove. $5.

To make
The Soft Machine
even less coherent
than his grotesque
Naked Lunch,
William Burroughs
scissored up
his manuscript
and pasted it
back together
higgledy-piggledy
before turning it in
to his publishers.
Results:
a hallucinatory little non-book
whose most distinguishing feature
is a preoccupation with sodomy
and the dubious joys thereof.

Burroughs apologists
insist that
there are plot
and Profound Meaning
imbedded in the book,
but only a cultist
will find them.

ARTICLE VII

The Ratification
of the Conventions
of nine States
shall be sufficient
for the Establishment
of this Constitution
between the States
so ratifying
the Same.

Constitution
Act or process
of constituting;
esp., act of enacting,
establishing,
or appointing.
An authoritative
or established
law or custom.
The aggregate
of the physical
and vital powers
of an individual;
also, temperament
or disposition.
Natural structure
or texture.
The mode
of organization
of a social group.

The fundamental
organic law
or principles
of government
of a nation,
state,
society,
or other organized
body of men,
embodied
in written documents,
or implied
in institutions
and customs;
also, a written instrument
embodying
such organic law.

Don't disturb
your Savings account
or cash your Savings Bonds
to meet tax payments.
Once used,
chances are
you will never
put the money back.
With a Personal Loan
from Manufacturers Hanover,
you can pay
your taxes in full,

and repay the loan
in 12 equal
monthly installments.

The solution
solidifies
at low temperatures
but liquefies readily
when warmed,
retaining
its potency.

I'm writing
this letter
as my last one.
You've probably
already received word
that I'm dead
and that the government
wishes to express
its deepest regrets.
Believe me,
I didn't want
to die.

Done in Convention,
by the Unanimous Consent
of the States present,
the Seventeenth Day of September,
in the Year of our Lord
one thousand seven hundred and eighty-seven,
and of the Independence

of the United States of America
the Twelfth.
In Witness
whereof We
have hereunto
subscribed
our Names.

John Giorno
(1966)

NOTES

PREAMBLE

Lines	1–15	The Constitution of the United States.
"	16–21	New York Times: Sun, Oct 31, 1965, Section 11, p 3.
"	22–40	New York Times: Sun, Oct 31, 1965, p 1, col 6.

ARTICLE I
Section 1

Lines	1–8	The Constitution of the United States.
"	9–22	New York Times: Wed, Apr 13, 1966, p 1, col 2.
"	23–29	Eastern Airlines boarding pass.
"	30–35	New York Times: Wed, Apr 13, 1966, p 1, col 2.

ARTICLE I
Section 2

Lines	1–12	The Constitution of the United States.
"	13–17	Reader's Digest: British Edition, Vol 88, No 529, May 1966, p 13.
"	18–27	New York Journal American: Wed, Apr 13, 1966, p 1, col 8.
"	28–35	New York World-Telegram & Sun: Thurs, Apr 14, 1966, p 1, col 8.
"	36–45	New York World-Telegram & Sun: Thurs, Apr 14, 1966, p 1, col 8.
"	46–49	New York World-Telegram & Sun: Thurs, Apr 14, 1966, p 1, col 3.
"	50–60	The Wall Street Journal: Tues, May 3, 1966, p 2, col 6.
"	61–70	New York World-Telegram & Sun: Thurs, Apr 14, 1966, p 1, col 1.
"	71–80	The Constitution of the United States.
"	81–86	New York Journal-American: Fri, Apr 15, 1966, p 1, col 8.
"	87–105	New York World-Telegram & Sun: Thurs, Apr 14, 1966, p 1, col 4.
"	106–149	The Constitution of the United States.
"	150–159	New York World-Telegram & Sun: Thurs, Apr 14, 1966, p 1, col 5.

" 160–167 New York World-Telegram & Sun: Thurs, Apr 14, 1966, p 1, col 8.

" 168–181 New York World-Telegram & Sun: Thurs, Apr 14, 1966, p 1, col 5.

" 182–189 New York World-Telegram & Sun: Thurs, Apr 14, 1966, p 1, col 8.

" 190–197 New York World-Telegram & Sun: Thurs, Apr 14, 1966, p 1, col 5.

" 198–206 New York World-Telegram & Sun: Wed, Apr 13, 1966, p 1, col 8.

" 207–213 The Constitution of the United States.

" 214–222 New York World-Telegram & Sun: Mon, Apr 11, 1966, p 1, col 8.

" 223–240 New York World-Telegram & Sun: Fri, Apr 22, 1966, p 1, col 4.

" 241–250 New York World-Telegram & Sun: Fri, Apr 22, 1966, p 1, col 1.

" 251–267 New York World-Telegram & Sun: Thurs, Apr 14, 1966, p 1, col 6.

" 268–283 New York Journal-American: Tues, Apr 12, 1966, p 1, col 3.

" 284–289 Long Island Railroad Time Table: Manhasset, effective Dec 15, 1959.

" 290–294 The Constitution of the United States.

" 295–313 New York World-Telegram & Sun: Thurs, Apr 14, 1966, p 2, col 4.

" 314–325 New York Times: Thurs, Apr 14, 1966, p 1, col 4.

" 326–330 New York World-Telegram & Sun: Thurs, Apr 14, 1966, p 2, col 4.

ARTICLE IV
Sections 1 and 2

Lines 1–17 The Constitution of the United States.

" 18–29 A Handbook of Information for Trial Jurors Serving in the Courts of the Counties of New York and the Bronx, p 3.

" 30–39 New York Journal-American: Mon, Mar 28, 1966, p 1, col 7.

" 40–46 The Constitution of the United States.

" 47–57 A Handbook of Information for Trial Jurors Serving in the Courts of the Counties of New York and the Bronx, p 3.

" 58–70 New York Journal-American: Mon, Mar 28, 1966, p 1, col 7.

" 71–74 New York Journal-American: Mon, Mar 28, 1966, p 1, col 1.

" 75–89 New York World-Telegram & Sun: Mon, Mar 28, 1966, p 2, col 4.

" 90–99 New York Journal-American: Mon, Mar 28, 1966, p 1, col 7.

" 100–118 The Constitution of the United States.

" 119–125 New York World-Telegram & Sun: Mon, Mar 28, 1966, p 1, col 3.

" 126–129 Grammar & Style: Waddell, The Dryden Press, New York, 1951, p 109.

" 130–137 New York World-Telegram & Sun: Mon, Mar 28, 1966, p 1, col 4.

" 138–155 A Handbook of Information for Trial Jurors Serving in the Courts of the Counties of New York and the Bronx, p 4.

" 156–175 Harper's Bazaar: October, 1965, p 70.

" 176–184 New York World-Telegram & Sun: Mon, Mar 28, 1966, p 1, col 3.

" 185–201 Nabisco Corp: oatmeal cookies label.

" 202–208 New York World-Telegram & Sun: Mon, Mar 28, 1966, p 1, col 5.

" 209–224 The Constitution of the United States.

" 225–234 The City of New York: traffic summons.

" 235–240 New York World-Telegram & Sun: Mon, Mar 28, 1966, p 1, col 4.

" 241–265 A Handbook of Information for Trial Jurors Serving in the Courts of the Counties of New York and the Bronx, p 13.

" 266–268 New Cyclophonic Miracles Sound Recording; recorded and manufactured especially for Reader's Digest by the Radio Corporation of America.

ARTICLE IV

Sections 3 and 4

Lines 1–19 The Constitution of the United States.

" 20–27 MD-Medical Magazine: Vol 9, No 10, Oct, 1965, p 53.

" 28–42 The Big View: Vol 1, No 4, Dec, 1962, p 9.

" 43–47 Grammar and Style: Waddell, The Dryden Press, New York, 1951, p 148.

" 48–52 New York Journal American: Mon, Mar 28, 1966, p 1, col 7.

" 53–84 Words and Idioms: Logan Pearsall Smith, Constable and Co., London, 1925, p 13.

" 85–89 Hempstead Bank: matchbox cover.

" 90–99 New York World-Telegram & Sun: Mon, Mar 28, 1966, p 1, col 4.

"	100–131	The Constitution of the United States.
"	132–140	U.S. government contract bid.
"	141–148	New York Daily News: Fri, Jan 15, 1965, p 2.
"	149–176	Time Magazine: Atlantic Edition, April 8, 1966, p 72.

ARTICLE VII

Lines	1–10	The Constitution of the United States.
"	11–47	Webster's New Collegiate Dictionary: 1951, p 178.
"	48–62	Manufacturers Hanover Trust: business reply card.
"	63–69	Tinactin, brand of tolnaftate solution: label.
"	70–81	New York World-Telegram & Sun: Tues, Mar 8, 1966, p 2
"	82–95	The Constitution of the United States.
"	96	Birth Certificate: New York, Dec 4, 1936.

(1966)

PORNOGRAPHIC POEM

Seven Cuban
army officers
in exile
were at me
all night.
Tall,
sleek,
slender
Spanish types
with smooth dark
muscular bodies
and hair
like wet coal
on their heads
and between their legs.
I lost count
of the times
I was fucked
by them
in every conceivable
position.
At one point
they stood
around me
in a circle
and I had
to crawl
from one crotch
to another
sucking
on each cock
until it was hard.

When I got all
seven up
I shivered
looking up
at those erect pricks
all different lengths
and widths
and knowing
that each one
was going up
my ass hole.
Every one
of them
came
at least twice
and some three times.
Once they put me
on the bed
kneeling,
one fucked me
in the behind,
another in the mouth,
while I jacked off
one
with each hand
and two
of the others
rubbed
their peckers
on my bare feet
waiting
their turns
to get
into my can.
Just when I thought

they were all spent
two of them
got together
and fucked me
at once.
The positions
we were in
were crazy
but with two
big fat
Cuban cocks
up my ass
at one time
I was
in paradise.

(1965)

CAPSULE

Enter
at South Gate.

On tour,
in candy-stripe shirts
and pressed wheat jeans,
the Beach Boys
look like anything
but a choir.

The poets
arrive
at the foot
of a tall tower.

Eighteen skydivers,
buffeted
by a 58-mile-an-hour wind,
parachuted
20,000 feet
into Lake Erie today.

To be read
or chanted,
with the heavy
buzzing bass
of fire-engines
pumping.

They walk
along the line
from the Ford Pavilion,

and then walk
through it
to look
at the Lincoln automobile
which is displayed
outside
the Ford Theatre.

Look
at the Falcon.

In this passage
the reading
or chanting
is shriller
and higher.

"Something
happened
and they went
off course,"
he said.

Pick up
Ford literature.

Songs like
"Heroes and Villains,"
are fragmented
by speeding up
or slowing down
their verses
and refrains.

The skydivers
jumped
from the B-25
Liberator
and plunged
into the choppy,
rough waters—
10 miles
off their course.

Look
at the Thunderbird.

An organ,
breathing heavily
over voices
hushed in wonder,
created
the elusive sound
that has been associated
with the Beach Boys
ever since.

Two
were known dead,
two were rescued
and 14
were still missing
in the chilly
murky waters.

Salt-water marshes
are in effect
natural breakwaters,

with the resiliency
of the millions
of stalks
of cord grass
serving
to mitigate
the shock
of pounding waves.

They have observed
two twinkling
points of light
at its top,
and now, from far
across the marsh,
they see
the flicker
of an answering beacon.

To be read
or chanted
in a heavy bass.

The boat
sets out
across the marsh,
bound for
the city
of Dis.

Shriller
and higher.

The effect
is like viewing

the song
through a spinning
prism.

One
of the survivors,
Robert Coy, 23,
told the highway patrol:
"We could see
nothing
but clouds.
I was shocked
and flabbergasted
to see that
I was over
the lake.
We assumed
we were over
the field."

Leave
the pavilion.

The listener
is thrown
into a vast
musical machine
of countless
working gears,
each spinning
in its own orbit.

Heavy bass.

Bears,
in two separate
attacks
20 miles apart,
killed two
19-year-old girls
in sleeping bags
in Glacier
National Park
early today
and seriously injured
an 18-year-old boy.

They walk slowly
and talk with
each other.

Two boys
were mauled
by a bear today
in a Forest Service
campground
southeast of Glacier
National Park,
where grizzlies
attacked and killed
two coeds
two weeks ago.

The muddy creature
reaches out
to grasp
the boat,
but Virgil
thrusts him away.

They walk
on through the line
and to the Gas Pavilion.

With a climax
of whispered
mourning.

"The waves
were over
my head
and water
swishing
into my mouth,"
Coy said.

In the Natural
Gas Pavilion.

A structure
erected
over a depression
or an obstacle,
as over a river,
roadway,
railway, etc.,
carrying
a roadway
for passengers,
vehicles, etc.

They look
at the absorption
water chiller.

In "Getting Hungry,"
two enchanting melodies
are so dissimilar
that the song
jerks like a car
trying unsuccessfully
to change gears.

Two major
forest fires
in Glacier National Park—
including the largest
in its history—
were virtually contained
within fire lines today,
with the help
of the Air Force,
the National Guard,
private loggers
and crews made up
of 250 Eskimos
from southern Alaska.

Rebel angels
who are guarding
the ramparts
of the city
refuse admission
to the poets.

The man takes
movie shots
in the pavilion.

(1966)

FREAKED

The tiny figure
dressed in bright green
was almost lost
atop the colossal concrete plug
that is Glen Canyon Dam.
As far away
as the eye could see
was an empty landscape
of savage splendor,
bright red,
treeless,
dotted with sculptured
sandstone spires
and flat-topped mesas.

A diameter
divides
a circle
into two
equal parts.

"I am proud
that man is here,"
said Mrs. Lyndon Baines Johnson,
speaking into the microphones
before the other tiny figures
thickly clustered along the top
of the 710-foot-high dam.

If a chord
divides a circle
into two equal parts,
then it is a diameter.

"Man is here,"
echoed the sheer walls
of the Colorado River gorge,
sealed now,
and named Lake Powell
with its blue-black waters,
hundreds of feet deep.
It is backed up
for 186 miles.

A point
is outside,
on,
or inside
a circle
depending on whether
its distance
from the center
is greater than,
equal to,
or less than
the radius.

"Any American who flies,
as I did today,
from sea to shining sea,
is newly impressed
with the beauties
of this vast country

and newly resentful
of the scars
that mar
its surface," she said.

Radii
of the same
or equal circles
are equal.

"I hope
it will be protected
from bumper-to-bumper traffic
and remain always
a place of peace,"
she told the crowds
on the windy promontory
overlooking the Pacific Ocean.

Diameters
of the same
or equal circles
are equal.

She can't come
to you for truth,
but you can
reach her.

In the same
or equal circles,
equal central angles
have equal arcs.

A well-dressed woman
who collapsed
and died
Wednesday evening
after chasing
a bicycle-riding youth
who had snatched
her purse,
was identified
yesterday
as Mrs. Betty Weiner, 62,
of 1520 Sheridan Ave, Bronx.

In the same
or equal circles,
equal arcs
have equal
central angles.

He stood up
and screeched
with pain.
His legs
were on fire.

In the same
or equal circles,
equal chords
have equal arcs.

"Oh, no,
I'm burning!"
the man screamed.

In the same
or equal circles,
equal arcs
have equal chords.

He turned around
a couple of times
and then began running
down the hill
toward the company.
When he moved
the phosphorus
drained down
his legs
and began to hiss
and spurt
and pop
as the chemical reaction
gnawed at his limbs.

A diameter
perpendicular
to a chord
bisects
the chord
and its arcs.

"Somebody shoot me!"
he yelled uncontrollably.

"Please shoot me,
shoot me!"

A perpendicular
bisector
of a chord
passes through
the center
of the circle.

Close circuit TV
helps us stop smoke
before it starts.

In the same
or equal circles,
equal chords
are equally distant
from the center.

Male Connector
Female Connector
Male Connector
Female Connector
Half Stage Plug
Male Connectors
Stage Plug
3 Way Branch Off

May we have
your name
for our mailing list?

(1966)

HEAD

Drop out
of school now
and that's what
they'll call you
all your working life.

ULTRA Turquoise
ULTRA Emerald
ULTRA Shamrock

Turn in
your heavyweight cycle
and we'll turn you
loose on
the X-6 Hustler.

ULTRA Blue
ULTRA Violet
ULTRA Fuchsia

Leisurely thieves
with long plumbing experience
have stripped
every flushing valve
from the lavatories
of Public School 157
and every drinking fountain valve
from the corridors.

Copper Bronze

Small teardrop
chrome gas tank,
high exhaust,
new colors
and glistening chrome job
give the Barracuda
a custom bike look.

ULTRA Red

Who'd hire
mentally retarded people?

ULTRA Orange
ULTRA Yellow

An unemployed
41-year-old Brooklyn man
with a record of drug convictions
collapsed in Brooklyn Criminal
court yesterday
while being arraigned
on a homicide charge
in the strangulation
of his 68-year-old mother.

ULTRA Gold

Is this the way
to train
a champ?

Sub-Marine Copper Bronze

In the beginning
a little loving fun
is just right.

ULTRA Olive
ULTRA Copper

Like how to develop
the Featherbed Frame
with Road-holder Fork.
Only 33 pounds
but solid
as a battleship
The most copied frame
in racing.

Vinyl Red

Like the rugged A.M.C.
gearbox
and a clutch
that can take
all sorts of punishment.

Copper Red
Sub-Marine Red

Like brawny breaks
with full wide alloy hubs
for extra safety.

Sub-marine Green

Adolescent girls
are placed
in Bellevue's
adult wards,
with prostitutes,
drug addicts
and alcoholics,
with whom they shower
two at a time
in small stalls,

ULTRA Brown
ULTRA Russet
ULTRA Charcoal

and then dry themselves
on a "community sheet,"
lacking towels.

Sometimes I think
we actually spend
more of our time
screening prospects
that we do selling.

ULTRA Jet Black

Police are hunting
two sadistic youths
who reportedly drenched
three homeless men
with kerosene
and turned them
into human torches.

(1967)

GIVE IT TO ME, BABY

About midnight
someone
entered
the room
and felt
his way
to where
he heard me
breathing.

3–5 Bedrooms

Blend tomato paste,
salad dressing,
water
and Worcestershire.

He quietly
took off
his clothes
and slipped
into bed.

Snipers
and arsonists
made daring
daylight raids
in the heart
of Detroit's
riot area
late today.

2 ½–3 ½ Baths

He put
his arm
over me
and felt
my cunt.

Toss
with steak
cubes
to coat.

Four persons
were wounded
in a wild
gun battle
outside
a police
station house
on the city's
riot-ravaged
West Side.

He opened
the lips
and rubbed
about the clitoris
and then tried
to push
his finger up.

Basement

Cover
and marinate
few hours
or overnight
in refrigerator.

On television sets
throughout the city,
football teams
seem to have
33 players
and 3 coaches.

It looked
very red
and open,
while the rich juices
of her previous fuck
trickled down
her bottom.

Ed Sullivan
comes on
as twins.

A Negro
teen-ager
in a green shirt
jumped in
through the shattered
window,
selected
a shiny new
straw hat,
put it on,
and strode away

with a grin
on his face.

He took out
his prick,
and held it
in his hand,
while he opened
the lips
of my cunt.

Alternate
steak,
onion,
green pepper
and tomatoes
on four
15-inch
skewers.

It was
the largest prick
I ever saw,
and had
a tremendous head.

Focus 12
is a handsome,
compact unit
that attaches easily
to any TV set.

The huge prick
was in
my cunt.

Oversized
2 car
Side Entry
Garage
with blacktop
Driveway
and storage area.

Place
on broiler
pan.

Roving bands
of defiant young
Negroes,
some wearing
shiny new clothes
that they had stolen,
pranced through
the debris-cluttered
streets
in the heavily Negro
Central Ward.

2-Zone
Hot Water
Heat

Brush
meat
with marinade
and vegetables
with oil.

The huge
prick
was in
my cunt.

Expansion level
for 2 extra Bedrooms
and Bath

I felt it
everywhere.

When you got
a job to do,
reach for something
good to chew,
chewing helps you
stand the pace,
anytime
and any place.

I grasped
her buttocks.

Broil
4–5 inches
from heat
15–20 minutes.

I lifted
her up.

Flames
and smoke
visible
from the downtown

Loop
billowed
from burning buildings
in a West Side slum.

As he arose
I clasped
my arms
around his neck,
and crossed
my legs
over his back.

Hi Ho Hey Hey
chew your little
troubles away.

While firemen
worked,
looters
carried off
furniture,
appliances,
television sets
and liquor.

Hi Ho Hey Hey,
chew Wrigley's
Spearmint Gum.

"Give it
to me,
baby!
Oh, man!
Give it

to me
all the way!
Fuck me,
fuck me,
fuck me,
and don't
ever stop!"

It focuses
the image
of the channel
you select
by shielding
the direct signal
from all outside
interference.

Some youth
hurled bricks
at firemen.

Antique Brick
and Rustic
Hand Split
Shingle
Exterior

Two suction fans
lift carpet
while beater bars
loosen dirt
and revolving
brushes
whisk dirt

into fan jet
suction stream.

Turn
and baste
often.

Ranches
and Colonials
from $35,990

Work
goes faster,
smoother too,
life
seems brighter
when you chew.

Every nerve
within me
thrilled
with rapture,
as he shot
into my vitals
a stream
of gushing
sperm.

Hi Ho Hey Hey
chew
Wrigley's
Spearmint Gum.

A "loud
thunderous
explosion
and a flash
of brilliant light"
jarred
this small
northeastern
Oklahoma town
early today
as a long-abandoned
zinc mine
collapsed,
swallowing
two houses
and five cars
and injuring
five people.

On Full
1 Acre
Estates

(1968)

FLAVOR GRABBER

Watch
the flavor grabber
game.

An experiment
I am about
to test
is to take
two tapes
which may
or may not be
of the same
content.

I could see
he had
a hard-on
and a big one
that reached
nearly
to the top
of his high
boots.

How many
L & M
cigarettes
are grabbed
in the next
50 seconds?

The cop
started
to call me
filthy names
and was slapping
my face.

Prepares boys,
grades 8–12,
for leading
colleges,
adult life.

Watch,
there goes
a flavor grabber.

Then they both
stripped
and the cop
shoved
his huge dong
into my asshole
without even
spitting on it.

Now started
running
tape 1
forward
from the beginning
and tape 2
start
at the end
and flash back

not playing
backwards.

There's another
flavor grabber.

As I screamed
in pain
the mechanic
pissed
all over
both of us.

Promotes
initiative,
leadership,
courtesy,
poise,
character growth.

When you grab
hold
of an L & M,
you grab hold
of flavor,
good round flavor,
never sharp,
never flat.

He shot
a load
into my ass
that felt
like a pint.

The scene
in the centre
depicts
the Buddha
throwing away
a mad elephant.

You understand
but simply
the last
of the tape
played first
so the two tapes
are simultaneously
running backwards
and forwards
past
each other.

He no sooner
pulled
it out
than the mechanic
ran his 13 inches
into my flaming
butt
right up
to the balls.

Outstanding
faculty,
facilities.
Fully accredited.

Good round flavor
you just can't get
in any other filter
cigarette.

Sword
with gilded scabbard
mounted
with coral orbs.

He fucked me
savagely
and when
I cried out
in pain,
the cop
shoved
the mechanic's
dirty jockey shorts
into my mouth.

All sports.
ROTC.
Artillery,
Cavalry,
Infantry,
Band.

Grab,
get hold
of an L & M.

After the mechanic
came,
he pulled out

real quick
so that it felt
like my guts
would come out
with it.

Then when
tape 1
comes
to the end
run backwards
and when tape 2
comes
to the beginning
run forward.

1500 acres
on lake.
Scholarships.
Catalog.

Be a flavor grabber.

(1969)

Cut out the cards.

Make a deck and shuffle thoroughly.

Hold the deck with both hands and think of a question.

Shuffle the deck three times. Cut the deck three times from left to right.

Lay out all the cards face down on a table. Concentrate on them and pick five cards. Place the first on the left, the second on the right, then the top, bottom, and center. Turn them up one at a time.

Andy Warhol
Andy Warhol,
the artist
the artist
who brought
a bewildering
who brought a bewildering
new dimension
new dimension
to American
pop culture
to American pop culture
through his films
through his films,
sculptures
and painting
sculptures and painting,
was shot
was shot
and critically
wounded
and critically wounded
in his film studio
in his film studio
yesterday afternoon
yesterday afternoon.

The acceptance
of this ticket
The acceptance of this ticket
is an act
of agreement
is an act of agreement
between the holder thereof
between the holder thereof
and the management
of this Hotel
and the management of this
Hotel
that he will in no way
consider
that he will in no way consider
the latter
responsible
the latter responsible
for the loss
for the loss
of any or all
articles
of any or all articles
which he may leave
in his room
which he may leave in this room.

To get him
to purify
To get him to purify
himself
completely
himself completely
she offered him
a bowl
she offered him a bowl
of putrid food
of putrid
food.

The Prince
The Prince,
repulsed
by its odour
repulsed by its odour
threw it
away
threw it away.

"You still
harbour
You still harbour
the concept
the concept
of good
and bad
of good and bad
in you
in you,"
the Dakini
told him
the Dakini
told him angrily
angrily.

He attained
perfection
He attained
perfection
and his fame
and his fame
spread
far
and wide
spread
far and wide.

The umbilical
cord
The umbilical cord
was then carefully
taken
was then carefully taken
and buried
in enemy
territory
and buried
in enemy territory
so that some attraction
would draw
so that some attraction
would draw
the child
there
the child there
in warfare
in warfare.

His symbols
of royalty
His symbols of royalty
are beyond
price
are beyond price:
a pearl-embroidered
silk cape
a pearl-embroidered silk cape,
a gold girdle
a gold girdle
with an egg-size
emerald buckle
with an egg-size emerald
buckle,
the "all-conquering" sword
the "all-conquering" sword
jewelled
with emeralds
jewelled with emeralds
diamonds diamonds,
and rubies
and rubies,
and a gold
scepter
and a gold scepter.

The line
The line
that tied
the astronaut
that tied the astronaut
to his orbiting
capsule
to his orbiting capsule—
immediately
dubbed
immediately dubbed
"the umbilical
cord
the umbilical cord"—
had a thin
gold-coating
had a thin gold-coating
that reflected
that reflected most
most of the sun's
of the sun's
heat
heat.

Three
South Vietnamese
Three South Vietnamese
105-mm. artillery
shells
105-mm. artillery shells
that had plunged
that had plunged
through the graceful
pagoda-style
roof
through the graceful
pagoda-style roof
lay
unexploded
lay unexploded
on the throne-room
floor
on the throne-room floor.

from **JOHN GIORNO'S TAROT CARDS**

In human
beings
In human beings
he has shown
that electrical
stimulation
he has shown
that electrical stimulation
of key spots
in the brain
of key spots in the brain
can evoke fear
can evoke fear
or reactions
or reactions
that can be
interpreted
that can be interpreted
as friendliness
as friendliness.

"It is important
to recognize
It is important to recognize
that as a result
of his relaxed,
euphoric state
that as a result of his relaxed,
euphoric state,
the individual
the individual
who uses marijuana
who uses marijuana
is more
suggestible
is more suggestible;
he is therefore
more easily
he is therefore more
easily influenced
influenced
to believe
something
to believe something
which may be a clear
distortion
which may be a clear distortion."

Beginning
Beginning
at a little before noon
at a little before noon,
the gangs
punched passerbys
the gangs punched passerbys,
looted
street stands
looted street stands,
vandalized
autos
vandalized autos,
smashed scores of office building
windows
smashed scores
of office building windows
and rained
bottles
and rained bottles,
rocks rocks
and jagged
pieces of glass
and jagged pieces of glass
on the police
on the police.

Police
searching
Police searching
for runaway
for runaway
17-year-old
socialite
17-year-old socialite
Marion
Biddle Wood
Marion Biddle Wood
today sought
for questioning
today sought for questioning
two "hippie type"
servants
two "hippie type" servants
fired
by her mother
fired by her mother
shortly before
her disappearance
shortly before her disappearance
nearly five
days ago
nearly five days ago.

The prisoners'
hearts
The prisoners' hearts
were cut out
were cut out,
and their skins
were removed
and worn
and their skins
were removed and worn
in a grisly
dance
in a grisly dance
by their captors
or the priests
by their captors
or the priests.

The heartbeat
The heartbeat
of a 30-year-old
woman
of a 30-year-old woman
who had been
pronounced
dead
who had been pronounced
dead
was restored
later
was restored later
by a morgue
attendant
by a morgue attendant.

After
she was taken
After she was taken
to the morgue
to the morgue,
William Taylor,
an attendant
William Taylor, an attendant,
noticed
noticed
"a contraction
of the throat
a contraction of the throat"
and applied
mouth-to-mouth
and applied
mouth-to-mouth
resuscitation
resuscitation.

"Please
pay attention
to me
Please
pay attention to me,
please
love me
please love me,
please
save me
please save me."

The fact
The fact
that 9.9
people
per 1,000
that 9.9 people
per 1,000
are taking
nuptial vows
are taking nuptial vows
this year
this year
compared
with 8.5
in 1962
compared with 8.5
in 1962
is an important
statistic
is an important statistic
underlying
a boom
underlying a boom
in the jewelry
business
in the jewelry business.

"Surely,
life
Surely, life
is a precarious
situation
is a precarious situation,"
Tricia Nixon
Tricia Nixon told
told
a news
conference
a news conference.
"You may get
killed
You may get killed
crossing
the street
crossing the street,
but if you dwell
on it
but if you dwell on it
you become morbid
you become
morbid."

Since weeping
and head
colds
Since weeping
and head colds
present
the same
medical
symptoms
present the same
medical symptoms,
he added
he added,
it is possible
that many colds
it is possible
that many colds
are "symbolically
expressed
tears"
are "symbolically
expressed tears."

The motor
vehicle
The motor vehicle
registered
as shown
registered as shown
on the face
of this card
on the face of this card
has been rejected
has been rejected.

July 12, 1968

Bill Copley
The Letter Edged in Black
435 West 23rd Street
New York, NY 10011

Dear Bill Copley:

Enclosing JOHN GIORNO'S TAROT CARDS for Evergreen.

Suggested format: they be printed on 6 facing pages (12 pages), on heavy clay-coated stock, each page in a different color (yellow, blue, red, green, purple, orange), and printed with Fortune Bold type in complementing ink. The yellow page printed with purple ink, the blue with orange, etc. A card back, to be designed by Les Levine, would be repeated on the backs of the card pages.

Yours truly,

John Giorno

222 Bowery New York, N. Y.

JOHNNY GUITAR

10	She said
10	tonelessly
9	She said tonelessly
9	that her 16-year-old
8	son,
8	John
7	that her 16-year-old son,
7	John,
6	had been brooding
	and withdrawn
Any scanning	
of the human	The hardest
organism	task
Any scanning	The hardest task
of the human organism	one can have
must be a probe	one can have
going through	is to continue
all its parts	to love
Cops	Twist
in blue helmets	off
Cops in blue helmets	Twist off
and short-sleeved	the claws
and short-sleeved blue shirts	the claws
blue shirts	
	must be a probe
had been brooding	going through
and withdrawn	all its parts
since his father	and will
committed	and will, accordingly
suicide	accordingly,
since his father	tend
committed suicide	to destroy
last November	the tissue
last November,	

	6
tend to destroy	5
the tissue	5
on its way	4
on its way.	4
	3
is to continue	3
to love	2
one's	2
one's	We have
fellows	ignition
fellows	We have ignition
despite	
all the reasons	but that mother
despite all the reasons	and son
he should not	but that mother and son
he should not.	had enjoyed
	an early morning
Cops	snack
with bare arms	
swinging	Crack
Cops	each claw
with bare arms swinging	Crack each claw
in the TV	with a nutcracker
lights	with a nutcracker
Permit	had enjoyed
lift-off	an early morning snack
Permit lift-off	and conversation
	and conversation
To hold	before each went
an organism	before each
To hold an organism	went to bed
stable	to bed.
stable	
while part	A primary
of it	trap
is being slowly	A primary trap
destroyed	is to succumb

As the police
reconstructed it
yesterday
As the police
reconstructed it yesterday
the youth
had slipped out
of the apartment

Beelzebuth
Beelzebuth
appears
sometimes
appears sometimes
in monstrous
forms
in monstrous forms,
sometimes
like a giant
cow

Separate
the tailpiece
Separate the tailpiece
from the body
from the body
by arching
the back
by arching the back
until it cracks
until it cracks

while part of it
is being slowly
destroyed
with the intention
of re-creating it
with the intention

is to succumb
to invitations
to hate
to invitations to hate.

The Eagle
and Jaguar
Warriors
The Eagle and Jaguar
Warriors
were elite
orders

We have
lift-off
We have lift-off

We hugged
and kissed
We hugged and kissed
one another
for awhile

in the TV lights
while they went
for the head
with their clubs
while they went
for the head
with their clubs,
or for any place
below
the belt

the youth had slipped out
of the apartment
without
his mother's
knowledge

of re-creating it
out of other
material
elsewhere

one another for awhile
and then the phone
rang
and then the phone rang
on the bedside
table
on the bedside table.

This is launch
control
This is launch control

or for any place
below
the belt
they could
reach
they could reach.

There are those
who appoint
one
There are those
who appoint one
their executioners
their executioners.

Bend
back
Bend back
and break
the flippers
off

without
his mother's knowledge
and wandered alone

were elite orders;
and there were
many other
orders
and there were many
other orders
each of which

sometimes
like a giant cow,
at times
like a he-goat
at times like a he-goat,
with a long tail
with a long
tail.

and wandered
alone
through
the night-time
streets
through the night-time
streets,

We have cleared
the tower
We have cleared the tower

Sometimes
Sometimes
for the sake
of safety
of others

<table>
<tr><td align="right">and break</td><td>for the sake of safety</td></tr>
<tr><td align="right">the flippers off</td><td>of others</td></tr>
<tr><td align="right">tailpiece</td><td>it is necessary</td></tr>
<tr><td align="right">tailpiece</td><td>to act</td></tr>
<tr><td></td><td></td></tr>
<tr><td align="right">Keith felt</td><td>At 4:30 AM</td></tr>
<tr><td align="right">the sudden</td><td>At 4:30 AM,</td></tr>
<tr><td align="right">rush</td><td>according</td></tr>
<tr><td align="right">Keith felt</td><td>to the police</td></tr>
<tr><td align="right">the sudden rush</td><td>charge</td></tr>
<tr><td align="right">of hot sperm</td><td>according</td></tr>
<tr><td align="right">of hot sperm</td><td>to the police charge</td></tr>
<tr><td align="right">travel</td><td>against him</td></tr>
<tr><td align="right">down</td><td>against him,</td></tr>
<tr><td align="right">his throat</td><td>he fired</td></tr>
<tr><td align="right"></td><td>a bullet</td></tr>
<tr><td align="right">Coming up</td><td></td></tr>
<tr><td align="right">on 2 minutes</td><td>A feeling</td></tr>
<tr><td align="right">Coming up on 2 minutes</td><td>A feeling</td></tr>
<tr><td align="right"></td><td>of strong</td></tr>
<tr><td align="right">he fired a bullet</td><td>personal</td></tr>
<tr><td align="right">from a high-powered</td><td>attachment</td></tr>
<tr><td align="right">rifle</td><td>of strong</td></tr>
<tr><td align="right">from a high-powered rifle</td><td>personal attachment</td></tr>
<tr><td align="right">that wounded</td><td>induced</td></tr>
<tr><td align="right">one rider</td><td>by sympathetic</td></tr>
<tr><td align="right">on a passing</td><td>understanding</td></tr>
<tr><td align="right">Long Island</td><td></td></tr>
<tr><td align="right">Rail Road</td><td>it is necessary to act,</td></tr>
<tr><td align="right">train</td><td>but it is not</td></tr>
<tr><td align="right"></td><td>necessary also</td></tr>
<tr><td align="right">When angry</td><td>to hate them</td></tr>
<tr><td align="right">When angry,</td><td>but it is not necessary</td></tr>
<tr><td align="right">he vomits fire</td><td>also to hate them.</td></tr>
<tr><td align="right">he vomits fire.</td><td></td></tr>
<tr><td align="right"></td><td>The crowd</td></tr>
<tr><td align="right">Mark</td><td>in the street</td></tr>
<tr><td align="right">2 minutes</td><td>The crowd in the street</td></tr>
<tr><td align="right">Mark 2 minutes</td><td>stood</td></tr>
<tr><td align="right"></td><td>with handkerchiefs</td></tr>
</table>

It is a sacrifice
It is a sacrifice
of the ego's
stability
of the ego's stability
and a surrender
and a surrender
to the extreme
uncertainty

travel down
his throat
as the huge cock
emptied
itself
as the huge cock
emptied itself
with spasm
after spasm
with spasm after spasm.

that wounded one rider
on a passing
Long Island
Rail Road train
and killed
another
and killed another,
a 31-year-old
father
a 31-year-old father
of three
children
of three children.

Inboard
engines
Inboard engines
have shut down
have shut down

over
their faces
stood with handkerchiefs
over their faces
in the tear gas

each
of which
wore
a special
uniform
wore
a special uniform.

Moving in
close
Moving in close
with 55-mm
with 55-mm
Auto-Micro-
Nikkor
lens

The police
gathered
into groups
The police
gathered into groups
and then ran
into the kids
and then ran into the kids
and swung
their clubs
and swung their clubs.

to the extreme uncertainty
of what
must seem
of what must seem
like a chaotic

***from* BALLING BUDDHA, 1970**

Two squadrons
of archers
Two squadrons of archers
in cotton
armour
in cotton armour,
carrying
lances
and shields

Insert
a fork
Insert a fork
where the flippers
broke off
where the flippers
broke off
and push
and push

riot
like a chaotic riot
of phantasmal forms
of phantasmal
forms.

Outboard
engines
have shut down
Outboard engines
have shut down

If there is any
saintly
quality
If there is any
saintly quality,
it is not
to forgive
it is not to forgive.

carrying
lances and shields,
approached
approached,
and each captain
drew up

He's got
ignition
He's got ignition
and he says
we're up
to thrust
and he says
we're up to thrust
on the second stage
on the second

in the tear gas
and they screamed
at the cops
and they screamed
at the cops.

"Pigs, Pigs, Pigs
Pigs, Pigs, Pigs."

and each captain drew up
a short
distance
a short distance
from where
we stood
from where we stood.

<table>
<tr><td align="right">stage</td><td>The swollen</td></tr>
<tr><td></td><td>head</td></tr>
<tr><td align="right">Lucifer</td><td>of the cock</td></tr>
<tr><td align="right">appears</td><td>The swollen head</td></tr>
<tr><td align="right">Lucifer appears</td><td>of the cock</td></tr>
<tr><td align="right">in the form</td><td>began</td></tr>
<tr><td align="right">and figure</td><td>to spit</td></tr>
<tr><td align="right">in the form and figure</td><td>forth</td></tr>
<tr><td align="right">of a fair boy</td><td></td></tr>
<tr><td align="right">of a fair</td><td>Half an hour</td></tr>
<tr><td align="right">boy.</td><td>later</td></tr>
<tr><td></td><td>Half an hour later</td></tr>
<tr><td align="right">Strong</td><td>young</td></tr>
<tr><td align="right">liking</td><td>Whitman</td></tr>
<tr><td align="right">Strong liking;</td><td>young Whitman,</td></tr>
<tr><td align="right">fondness</td><td>a slim</td></tr>
<tr><td align="right">fondness;</td><td>a slim,</td></tr>
<tr><td align="right">good</td><td>pink-cheeked</td></tr>
<tr><td align="right">will</td><td>youth</td></tr>
<tr><td align="right">good will;</td><td></td></tr>
<tr><td></td><td>Unhinge</td></tr>
<tr><td align="right">Auto-Micro-Nikkor</td><td>Unhinge</td></tr>
<tr><td align="right">lens</td><td>back</td></tr>
<tr><td align="right">on Nikon 5</td><td>from body</td></tr>
<tr><td align="right">on Nikon 5,</td><td>back from body</td></tr>
<tr><td align="right">Gary</td><td>This Contains</td></tr>
<tr><td align="right">Winegrand</td><td>the “Tom</td></tr>
<tr><td align="right">Gary Winegrand</td><td>Alley”</td></tr>
<tr><td align="right">photographed</td><td>or liver</td></tr>
<tr><td align="right">woman</td><td>This contains</td></tr>
<tr><td align="right">clerk</td><td>the “Tom Alley”</td></tr>
<tr><td></td><td>or liver</td></tr>
<tr><td align="right">The police</td><td></td></tr>
<tr><td align="right">seem to be</td><td>When angry</td></tr>
<tr><td align="right">re-grouping</td><td>When angry,</td></tr>
<tr><td align="right">The police</td><td>he seems</td></tr>
<tr><td align="right">seem to be-regrouping</td><td>red</td></tr>
<tr><td></td><td>he seems red.</td></tr>
</table>

***from* BALLING BUDDHA, 1970**

began
to spit forth
the warm
the warm,
sticky
fluid
sticky fluid,
covering
Keith's
bare
stomach
covering Keith's
bare stomach.

Only after
capturing
Only after capturing
a certain
number
a certain number
of enemies

out of other
material
elsewhere,
involves
a lowering
involves a lowering
of its degree
of activity

that the dead
that the dead
simply
continue
simply continue
their earthly
existence

pink-cheeked youth
with deep dark
eyes
with deep dark eyes,
was picked up
was picked up
by two railroad
policemen

That tower
has really
jettisoned
That tower
has really jettisoned

photographed
woman clerk
in store
in store
who had just
waited on him
who had just waited
on him.

by two railroad policemen
near the 43rd
Street
trestle
near the 43rd Street
trestle

That he was then
shot
That he was then shot
had nothing
to do
with us

a mile or so
east
a mile or so east
of the vast
Sunnyside
of the vast Sunnyside,
Queens
Queens,
train yards
train yards.

"The whole
world
is watching
The whole world
is watching,"
chants
the crowd
chants the crowd
on the side
on the side.

We're nearing
50 miles
altitude now
We're nearing
50 miles altitude now

their earthly existence
and do not know
and do not know
that they are disembodied
spirits
that they are disembodied
spirits.

had nothing
to do with us,
but only demonstrated
how incompetent

Even when
he grabbed
my testicles
Even when he grabbed
my testicles
with one hand
with one hand
and placed
the sharp edge
of the blade
against my flesh

We do know
We do know
that wherever
our reporters go
on the floor
that wherever
our reporters go
on the floor
they are followed
by unidentified
faceless
men

and about
60 miles
and about 60 miles
down
range
down range

and placed
the sharp edge
of the blade
against my flesh
with the other
with the other
I was certain
that this was
as far
as they would go
I was certain
that this was as far
as they would go.

It has been
shown
It has been shown
that outrushing
gas
from the sun
that outrushing gas
from the sun
—the "solar
wind"

the youth
telephoned
a friend and said
and said
"This is station
KEVD
This is station KEVD.
signing off
for the night
signing of for the night."

Nothing
Nothing;
no points
scored

of its degree
of activity
which in most cases
would destroy
life
which in most cases
would destroy life
in the tissue
in the tissue.

On Saturday
night
On Saturday night,
a detective said
a detective said,
the youth
telephoned
a friend

Astaroth
appears
Astaroth appears
black
black,
in human
shape
in human shape.

of enemies
could a man
join one
of these societies
could a man join
one of these societies.

by unidentified
faceless men
who attempt
to listen
who attempt to listen

no points scored;

Through radio
contact
Through radio contact
with vertical
beams
with vertical beams,
a plane
is guided

There was no
particular
significance
There was no particular
significance
to it
to it,
the detective said
the detective said,

They only
emerge
into consciousness
They only emerge
into consciousness
when personal
experiences
when personal experiences
have rendered them visible
have rendered them
visible.

to everything
they say
to everything they say.

but only demonstrated
how incompetent
and how mortal
he really was
and how mortal
he really was.

And then
I felt
that knife
and then I felt
that knife
slice
through my balls
slice through my balls.

And the persistent
chanting
And the persistent chanting
by the crowd
by the crowd
"The whole
world
is watching
The whole world
is watching."

the "solar wind"—
limits
the extent
limits the extent
of this magnetic
field
of this magnetic field.

(1968)

CUNT

Bare
gold
bullion
Bare
gold bullion,
scarlet
flounces
scarlet flounces,
below
below:

the golden-yellow
pubic
hair
the golden-yellow
pubic hair,
the thin
the thin,
moist
moist,
pink
pink
opened
lips
opened lips,
the clitoris
the clitoris,

It can be
a small
way
It can be
a small way
of paying
of paying
yourself

Bare
gold
bullion
Bare
gold bullion,
scarlet
flounces
scarlet flounces,
below
below:

the golden-yellow
pubic
hair
the golden-yellow
pubic hair,
the thin
the thin,
moist
moist,
pink
pink
opened
lips
opened lips,
the clitoris
the clitoris,

It can be
a small
way
It can be
a small way
of paying
of paying
yourself
back

back
yourself back
for all those
years

Real
Society
women
Real
Society women
are often
tanned
the year
round

In childhood
In childhood
we are taught
to do right
we are taught to do right
by the threat
that mother

outlining
the body
perfectly
outlining the body
perfectly
in mauve
and golden
arabesques
in mauve
and golden arabesques

Always
sets
Always sets
impossible

yourself back
for all those
years

Real
Society
women
Real
Society women
are often
tanned
the year
round

In childhood
In childhood
we are taught
to do right
we are taught to do right
by the threat
that mother

outlining
the body
perfectly
outlining the body
perfectly
in mauve
and golden
arabesques
in mauve
and golden arabesques

Always
sets
Always sets
impossible
standards

standards
impossible standards
for you
for you.

by the threat that mother
will withdraw
her love
will withdraw her love
if we do
wrong

with her fingers
and showed me
voluptuously
and showed me voluptuously
her young
girl's
womb
her young girl's
womb

for all those years
of struggle
it took
it took
to get where
you are
to get
where you are.

are often tanned
the year round
from riding
and playing
golf
from riding
and playing golf
and tennis

impossible standards
for you
for you.

by the threat that mother
will withdraw
her love
will withdraw her love
if we do
wrong

with her fingers
and showed me
voluptuously
and showed me voluptuously
her young
girl's
womb
her young girl's
womb

for all those years
of struggle
it took
it took
to get where
you are
to get
where you are.

are often tanned
the year round
from riding
and playing
golf
from riding
and playing golf
and tennis
and tennis

and tennis
wherever
the sun
shines

Doris Duke
Doris Duke,
who abhors
crowds
and publicity
who abhors
crowds and publicity,
was there
was there.

She moved it
closer
to my face
She moved it
closer to my face,

Controls
you
Controls you
by giving you
guilt
by giving you guilt.

The search
for the world's
The search for the world's
most romantic
bathing suit
most romantic bathing suit
ends
here
ends here,
above
above,

wherever
the sun
shines

Doris Duke
Doris Duke,
who abhors
crowds
and publicity
who abhors
crowds and publicity,
was there
was there.

She moved it
closer
to my face
She moved it
closer to my face,

Controls
you
Controls you
by giving you
guilt
by giving you guilt.

The search
for the world's
The search for the world's
most romantic
bathing suit
most romantic bathing suit
ends
here
ends here,
above
above,

she inserted
her two
middle fingers
she inserted
her two middle fingers,

Sixty
delicate
pink pads
Sixty delicate
pink pads
with a special
liquid
with a special liquid

As Marcia
entered
As Marcia entered
the flowering
hibiscus
tunnel
hibiscus tunnel
that led
to the door
of the restaurant

"Pull it out
a little
Pull it out
a little,"
she said
in a hoarse
whisper
she said
in a hoarse whisper,

Manufactures
incidents

she inserted
her two
middle fingers
she inserted
her two middle fingers,

Sixty
delicate
pink pads
Sixty delicate
pink pads
with a special
liquid
with a special liquid

As Marcia
entered
As Marcia entered
the flowering
hibiscus
tunnel
hibiscus tunnel
that led
to the door
of the restaurant

"Pull it out
a little
Pull it out
a little,"
she said
in a hoarse
whisper
she said
in a hoarse whisper,

Manufactures
incidents
Manufactures incidents

Manufactures incidents
in which you
are trapped
in which you are trapped
into hurting
his (or her)
into hurting his (or her)
feelings
feelings.

"I want
to see it
I want to see it
go in
again
go in again."

Lacquered-flower
tunic
Lacquered-flower tunic
belted
over pants
belted over pants,

and she felt
as if she were
in
and she felt as
if she were in
a remote
Hawaiian
jungle
a remote
Hawaiian jungle.

She already had
She already had,
according
to inside
estimates

in which you
are trapped
in which you are trapped
into hurting
his (or her)
into hurting his (or her)
feelings
feelings.

"I want
to see it
I want to see it
go in
again
go in again."

Lacquered-flower
tunic
Lacquered-flower tunic
belted
over pants
belted over pants,

and she felt
as if she were
in
and she felt as
if she were in
a remote
Hawaiian
jungle
a remote
Hawaiian jungle.

She already had
She already had,
according
to inside
estimates
according

according
to inside estimates,
somewhere
between
$15,000,000
and $18,000,000

Her sex
was like an overripe
tropical
fruit
Her sex
was like an overripe
tropical fruit,
streaming
with juice
streaming with juice.

two daughters
each
two daughters each
of Henry Ford 2d
of Henry Ford 2d
(Charlotte Niarchos
and Anne Uzielli
Charlotte Niarchos
and Anne Uzielli)

Makes
you pay
Makes you pay
for every ounce
of "affection"
for every ounce
of "affection."

That's mainly
because
That's mainly because
of "the contraceptive

to inside estimates,
somewhere
between
$15,000,000
and $18,000,000

Her sex
was like an overripe
tropical
fruit
Her sex
was like an overripe
tropical fruit,
streaming
with juice
streaming with juice.

two daughters
each
two daughters each
of Henry Ford 2d
of Henry Ford 2d
(Charlotte Niarchos
and Anne Uzielli
Charlotte Niarchos
and Anne Uzielli)

Makes
you pay
Makes you pay
for every ounce
of "affection"
for every ounce
of "affection."

That's mainly
because
That's mainly because
of "the contraceptive
revolution

revolution

out
to conquer
out to conquer
at dinner
at dinner
with vivid
Portuguese
embroidered
sleeves
with vivid Portuguese
embroidered sleeves.

Her body
shook
with convulsions
Her body shook
with convulsions.

of "the contraceptive
revolution"
—which "may yet
prove
—which "may yet prove
to be the greatest
revolution
to be the greatest revolution
in mankind's
history
in mankind's history,"
said Mrs. Clare Boothe Luce
said Mrs. Clare Boothe
Luce.

Everybody
loves
a winner
Everybody loves
a winner.

out
to conquer
out to conquer
at dinner
at dinner
with vivid
Portuguese
embroidered
sleeves
with vivid Portuguese
embroidered sleeves.

Her body
shook
with convulsions
Her body shook
with convulsions.

of "the contraceptive
revolution"
—which "may yet
prove
—which "may yet prove
to be the greatest
revolution
to be the greatest revolution
in mankind's
history
in mankind's history,"
said Mrs. Clare Boothe Luce
said Mrs. Clare Boothe
Luce.

Everybody
loves
a winner
Everybody loves
a winner.

Sealskin
tunic
Sealskin tunic
and wide-legged
pants
and wide-legged pants,
right
right,

I hold
my vaginal
lips
together
I hold
my vaginal lips
together
and let my urine
and let my urine
spurt
through
my pubic
hairs
spurt through
my pubic hairs

So was
Mrs. William
Woodward
So was Mrs. William
Woodward,
the dowager
who abides
the dowager who abides
in the Waldorf
Towers
in the Waldorf Towers;

"Fortunately
for women

Sealskin
tunic
Sealskin tunic
and wide-legged
pants
and wide-legged pants,
right
right,

I hold
my vaginal
lips
together
I hold
my vaginal lips
together
and let my urine
and let my urine
spurt
through
my pubic
hairs
spurt through
my pubic hairs

So was
Mrs. William
Woodward
So was Mrs. William
Woodward,
the dowager
who abides
the dowager who abides
in the Waldorf
Towers
in the Waldorf Towers;

"Fortunately
for women
Fortunately for women

Fortunately for women,
her body
is still
a trap
her body
is still a trap

First
"loves" you
First "loves" you—
then destroys you
then destroys you.

if we do wrong,
but as we get
older
but as we get older,
our anxiety
about parental
disapproval

wherever
the sun shines—
and a perpetual
tan
and a perpetual tan
may lead
to a leathery
look

our anxiety
about parental
disapproval
gets transformed
into a generalized
fear
gets transformed
into a generalized fear
of supernatural
disaster

her body
is still
a trap
her body
is still a trap

First
"loves" you
First "loves" you—
then destroys you
then destroys you.

if we do wrong,
but as we get
older
but as we get older,
our anxiety
about parental
disapproval

wherever
the sun shines—
and a perpetual
tan
and a perpetual tan
may lead
to a leathery
look

our anxiety
about parental
disapproval
gets transformed
into a generalized
fear
gets transformed
into a generalized fear
of supernatural
disaster
of supernatural disaster.

of supernatural disaster.

the astronaut's
body
the astronaut's body
is as awkward
and encumbered
in the space
suit
is as awkward
and encumbered
in the space suit
as the body
of a pregnant
woman
as the body
of a pregnant woman.

the astronaut's
body
the astronaut's body
is as awkward
and encumbered
in the space
suit
is as awkward
and encumbered
in the space suit
as the body
of a pregnant
woman
as the body
of a pregnant woman.

A yell
rose
A yell rose
out
of her open
mouth
out of her open
mouth.

A yell
rose
A yell rose
out
of her open
mouth
out of her open
mouth.

with billow-sleeved
with billow-sleeved
eggshell
crepe
eggshell crepe
plunged
to the navel
plunged to the navel
and cut
high
and cut high
on the legs
on the legs.

with billow-sleeved
with billow-sleeved
eggshell
crepe
eggshell crepe
plunged
to the navel
plunged to the navel
and cut
high
and cut high
on the legs
on the legs.

—if no longer
a baby
trap
—if no longer
a baby trap,
a man
trap
a man trap,"
she said
she said.

and of Alfred
Gwynne Vanderbilt
and of Alfred Gwynne
Vanderbilt
(Heidi
and Wendy
Heidi and Wendy),

Pucker it
for me
Pucker it for me
and let
a good fart
and let a good fart;"

within
the skin
within the skin
to help keep
the skin's
water-moisture
level
to help keep
the skin's
water-moisture level
high

—if no longer
a baby
trap
—if no longer
a baby trap,
a man
trap
a man trap,"
she said
she said.

and of Alfred
Gwynne Vanderbilt
and of Alfred Gwynne
Vanderbilt
(Heidi
and Wendy
Heidi and Wendy),

Pucker it
for me
Pucker it for me
and let
a good fart
and let a good fart;"

within
the skin
within the skin
to help keep
the skin's
water-moisture
level
to help keep
the skin's
water-moisture level
high

Passionate
"romances"
Passionate "romances"
that settle
down
that settle down
overnight
overnight
to domination
and exploitation
to domination
and exploitation.

high
to prevent
the formation
to prevent the formation
of pre-mature
age lines
of pre-mature age lines.

somewhere between
$15,000,000
and $18,000,000,
the happy
results
the happy results
of 20 years
as a superstar
of 20 years
as a superstar.

openly
plunged
openly plunged—
the neckline
the neckline
meets
at the waist

Passionate
"romances"
Passionate "romances"
that settle
down
that settle down
overnight
overnight
to domination
and exploitation
to domination
and exploitation.

high
to prevent
the formation
to prevent the formation
of pre-mature
age lines
of pre-mature age lines.

somewhere between
$15,000,000
and $18,000,000,
the happy
results
the happy results
of 20 years
as a superstar
of 20 years
as a superstar.

openly
plunged
openly plunged—
the neckline
the neckline
meets
at the waist
meets at the waist

meets at the waist
of a flounced
organza
skirt
of a flounced
organza skirt.

"Young men
still desire
Young men still desire
women
women
as much
as ever

Like a woman
being carted
to a delivery
room
Like a woman
being carted
to a delivery room,
the astronaut

I think
Marge
must have had
I think Marge
must have had
fifty
orgasms
fifty orgasms
at the last
party
at the last party,

the astronaut
must sit
(or lie)
still

of a flounced
organza
skirt
of a flounced
organza skirt.

"Young men
still desire
Young men still desire
women
women
as much
as ever

Like a woman
being carted
to a delivery
room
Like a woman
being carted
to a delivery room,
the astronaut

I think
Marge
must have had
I think Marge
must have had
fifty
orgasms
fifty orgasms
at the last
party
at the last party,

the astronaut
must sit
(or lie)
still
must sit

must sit
(or lie) still,
and go
where
he is being
sent
and go where
he is being sent.

as well as
such energetic
partygoers
as well as
such energetic partygoers
as Susan Stein
as Susan Stein
and the Robert Sculls
and the Robert Sculls,

may lead
to a leathery look,
with crinkled
squint
lines
around the eyes
with crinkled
squint lines
around the eyes.

as much as
ever,
even though
they don't
want
even though
they don't want
to marry them
as much
to marry them as much."

(or lie) still,
and go
where
he is being
sent
and go where
he is being sent.

as well as
such energetic
partygoers
as well as
such energetic partygoers
as Susan Stein
as Susan Stein
and the Robert Sculls
and the Robert Sculls,

may lead
to a leathery look,
with crinkled
squint
lines
around the eyes
with crinkled
squint lines
around the eyes.

as much as
ever,
even though
they don't
want
even though
they don't want
to marry them
as much
to marry them as much."

(1970)

ESPE—ELECTRONIC SENSORY POETRY ENVIRONMENTS

Balling Buddha

Gain Ground Gallery, New York.

A stereo tape of *Balling Buddha,* made using a Moog Synthesizer, was played continuously over 8 stereo speakers placed around the room (25' × 25').

A tent was made from an orange nylon parachute, 6 feet high at the center to 3 feet at the walls. A fan at the ceiling blew the orange nylon.

100 feet of electroluminescent tape in 12-foot lengths of red, yellow, blue, green were hung in the center of the tent at a 6-foot height and stretched out radially toward the audience. The 1 ¾ inch wide tape light conducts light and is connected to a Light Organ, an electronic device which analyses the light content of sound. The tape light responding in intensity and pitch to the sound from the recording tape. Brightness controlled by volume, color by pitch.

The floor was lined with piles of foam rubber cushions. 3 Time-Mist aerosol dispensers made the air smell of peeled oranges.

The text of *Balling Buddha* was given out.

from BALLING BUDDHA, 1970

I Want to Turn You On

Performed at The Bandshell in Central Park, New York, September 28, 1968.

A stereo Moog tape of the poems *Groovy & Linda, Rainbow Fire, Lucky Man, Purple Heart* was played through horn speakers around the bandshell. The light column (described in *Johnny Guitar*) was played in the center of the bandshell.

6 1,000-watt spotlights with red gels flooded the audience. Strawberry incense burning in 7 clay pots was carried out and placed among the audience.

Johnny Guitar

Performed at St. Mark's Church, New York, April 2, 1969.

A stereo Moog tape of the poems *Johnny Guitar* and *Cunt* was played through 6 stereo speakers around the church. It is 40 minutes in length and was played continuously from 7:30 to 11:30 PM. An 8-foot double light column was lashed to the cross above the altar. The light column contained 30 150-watt bulbs (4,500 watts) of red, yellow, blue, green and was connected to a Light Organ which analyses the light content of the sound from the recording tape. The light column responding in brightness to volume and color to pitch.

The church pews in the front half of the church had been removed and 3 dozen votive candles were placed in that space with cushions to sit on. 3 Time-Mist aersol dispensing units, which release odors at timed intervals, filled the church with the smell of chocolate candy. The church was flooded with 6 1,000-watt spotlights with amber gels.

A pitcher of LSD punch was on a table at the side of the altar. The audience was invited to help themselves. Each cup contained ¼ of a trip. 5 gallons of punch were given away.

In the Parish Hall in the back of the church, a birthday party was given for Anne Waldman. There was rock music, food, wine, grass soup, grass birthday cake, and 600 joints were given away. The audience moved from the reading to the party, back to the reading and to the party.

The text of *Johnny Guitar* published by The Poetry Project at St. Mark's was given out at the entrance.

Purple Heart

Performed at Sightsound Systems, a Festival of Arts & Technology, Ryerson Institute, Toronto, Canada, March 9 & 10, 1968.

A stereo Moog tape of the poems *Capsule, Cycle, Rose, Groovy & Linda, Give It to Me, Baby, Flavor Grabber, Chrome, Purple Heart* was played through 4 stereo speakers at the 4 corners of the 1,500-seat theater. Striplights were placed across the front of the stage facing the audience (24 150-watt bulbs alternating red, blue, green). The striplights were connected to a Light Organ.

A fog machine on stage sent banks of fog, blown by a fan, rolling out across the audience, filling the theater with fog. Frankincense and sandalwood were put in the fog machine. 6 followspots with changing color gels, placed around the theater, moved randomly through the fog. The instructions to the students operating the follow-spots was to move them slowly over the audience, focusing on anyone for as long as they wanted to.

Also performed at: St. Mark's Church, New York, April 17, 1968. Fairleigh-Dickinson University, Madison, N.J., July 6 & 7, 1968. The Architectural League of New York, February 14, 1968. (At The Architectural League, 3 soap bubble machines were used instead of the fog machine. The audience was flooded with thousands of soap bubbles. Chanel No. 5 was put in the soap bubble liquid.) The Fashion Institute of Technology, New York. (Strawberry essence was put in the fog machine and the audience was flooded with red spotlights.) State University of New York, New Paltz. Skowhegan School of painting & Sculpture, Skowhegan, Maine, August 25, 1968.

Chromosome

Performed at The School of Visual Arts, New York, November 17, 18, & 19, 1967.

A stereo Moog tape of the poems *Cycle, Rose, Flavor Grabber, Chrome* was played through stereo speakers on either side of the stage. The seats in the theater are blanked at a 45-degree angle and 2 follow-spots with changing color gels were moved randomly over the audience (instructions in *Purple Heart*).

Raspberry

Performed at The Loeb Student Center, N.Y.U., March 7, 1967.

A stereo tape of the poems *Leather, Outlaw, She Tasted Death, Head, Pornographic Poem* was played through speaker system built in the ceiling. All the seats were removed from the theater. 8 4-foot-long ultra-violet blacklights were hung along the 4 sides. 500 people walked around listening and doing numbers with each other in what looked like a fish tank of ultra-violet water.

Also performed at The Filmmakers Cinematheque, New York, July 7, 1967.

(1968–70)

"I LOOKED THE SOLDIER GUARDING ME IN THE EYE"

"I looked
I looked
the soldier
guarding
me
the soldier guarding me
straight
in the eye
straight in the eye
and said
and said
'Well
Well,
why
are you waiting
why are you waiting
to kiss
my hand
to kiss my hand?'"

(1970)

"WE TOLD THEM TO BOMB IT"

"We told
them
We told them
    We told
    them
    We told them
to bomb
it
to bomb it,
    to bomb
    it
    to bomb it,
to blow it
up
to blow it up
    to blow it
    up
    to blow it up.
And then
they blew it
up
And then they blew it up
    And then
    And then
    they blew it
    up
    they blew it up.
And we said
And we said
    And we said
    And we said
"My God,
they blew it
up
My God, they blew it up
    My God
    My God,
    they blew it
    up
    they blew it up!"

(1970)

SHE HALF-OPENED HER EYES

She half-opened
her eyes
She half-opened her eyes
and smiled
bitterly
and smiled bitterly.

"I'm just
working
I'm just working
on this
tune
on this tune,"
she mumbled
she mumbled
in her rusty
voice
in her rusty voice.

"I'm gonna
call
it
I'm gonna call it
something
like
this
something like this:
'I Just
Made
Love
I Just Made Love
to 25,000
People
to 25,000 People,
But I'm
Going
Home
But I'm Going Home
Alone
Alone.'"

Then
she went
Then she went
to sleep
to sleep.

(1970)

"THE VIETCONG TAKE THE TOADS"

"The Vietcong
The Vietcong
take
the toads

Take the toads,
tie
their mouths
tie their mouths
with string
with string
and throw
them
and throw
them
into our camp

into our camp.

When
they croak
When they croak,
our soldiers
mistake
the croaking
our soldiers
mistake the croaking
for men's
voices

for men's voices
and we open
fire
and we open fire."

(1970)

THE SHOUTING CONTINUED

The shouting
continued
The shouting continued:
"Put
the gun
down
Put the gun down!
Get
your hands
up
Get your hands up!
Get'em
up
Get'em up!
Get your hands
up
Get your hands up!
Get
over here
Get over here.
Up
against
the wall
Up against the wall!
Get against
the wall
Get against the wall!
You
in here
alone
You in here alone?
Freeze
Freeze!
Drop
the gun
Drop the gun.
O.K.
O.K.
O.K. O.K.
Move
along
Move along.
Come
along
Come along."

(1970)

THIS BOOK IS CANCER

I had cancer in my left ball, which had gotten to be the size of a lemon and rock hard, so 5 doctors at Memorial Hospital cut the ball off. The pathology report came back saying it contained 4 kinds of cancer: Teratoma, Clorial, Embryonal Cell, and Seminoma. They made this 12 inch gash down the middle of my stomach, ripped out all my intestines and whatever else was in the way, then cut out 50 lymph nodes running up my spine, stuffed all the intestines back in and sewed me up. The first 36 hours, even though they were shooting me up every 3 hours with Demerol, was white pain and hell fire. All in all it was my best tantric meditation. I sort of miraculously healed in a very short time, much to the surprise of the doctors who kept saying "We don't know what you're doing, but keep doing it!" and the nurses and the dying patients who kept moaning "John, say your meditation for me! John, say your meditation for me!" Memorial Hospital is this charnel ground, where people rotting with cancer come to die. To be in a bed next to a man who dies, to hear his last gasp, to know the moment he dies and hang on it, is pretty interesting.

Then I flew out to Snow Lion, a Buddhist meditation retreat, in the Grand Tetons, Wyoming, for Trungpa Rinpoche's seminar on Padma Sambava. We took hot saunas and ran out naked rolling in the snow, which totally brought life back to my half dead body. Now I feel absolutely healed. Although the result of the cancer has been cut out, I don't know if the cause of the cancer is gone. Anyway, they can have any other part of my body they want, and they can have the whole thing.

The poems in this book were written in 1970–72. On the book cover are photos from the pathology report of those cancerous cells in my left ball. As the cancer got started, grew, and was cut out in the same 2 year period in which the poems were written, I think there is some connection between the body that wrote them and the poems. You might say that both are the result of the same karma. As the images of the poems are found in any words I've seen or heard in every day life, coming into my sense inputs from newspapers, magazine, radio, TV, or books, you might also say the poems bear the same relationship to American karma. The images are American cancer cells. The poems are a biopsy. The reality of cancer transformed into words. The cause of suffering in the American body, pictures of New York hells and heavens with cocksucking hunger-ghosts and elephants inside our loves. Endless thought saturation making our minds into prisons for the survival of those poison pictures. It's what we're dying of America!

(1973)

VAJRA KISSES

<table>
<tr><td></td><td>When</td></tr>
<tr><td align="right">When</td><td>starting</td></tr>
<tr><td align="right">starting</td><td>on a journey</td></tr>
<tr><td align="right">on a journey</td><td>When starting on a journey</td></tr>
<tr><td align="right">When starting on a journey</td><td>they did not</td></tr>
<tr><td align="right">they did not</td><td>tell</td></tr>
<tr><td align="right">tell</td><td>they did not tell</td></tr>
<tr><td align="right">they did not tell</td><td>their party</td></tr>
<tr><td align="right">their party</td><td>their party</td></tr>
<tr><td align="right">their party</td><td>where</td></tr>
<tr><td align="right">where</td><td>they were</td></tr>
<tr><td align="right">they were</td><td>going</td></tr>
<tr><td align="right">going</td><td>where they were going</td></tr>
<tr><td align="right">where they were going</td><td>or how</td></tr>
<tr><td align="right">or how</td><td>long</td></tr>
<tr><td align="right">long</td><td>it would</td></tr>
<tr><td align="right">it would</td><td>take</td></tr>
<tr><td align="right">take</td><td>or how long it would take</td></tr>
<tr><td align="right">or how long it would take</td><td></td></tr>
<tr><td></td><td>He looked</td></tr>
<tr><td align="right">He looked</td><td>at himself</td></tr>
<tr><td align="right">at himself</td><td>He looked at himself</td></tr>
<tr><td align="right">He looked at himself</td><td>in the mirror</td></tr>
<tr><td align="right">in the mirror</td><td>above</td></tr>
<tr><td align="right">above</td><td>the sink</td></tr>
<tr><td align="right">the sink</td><td>in the mirror above the sink</td></tr>
<tr><td align="right">in the mirror above the sink</td><td>and grinned</td></tr>
<tr><td align="right">and grinned</td><td>and grinned</td></tr>
<tr><td align="right">and grinned</td><td></td></tr>
<tr><td></td><td>particular</td></tr>
<tr><td align="right">particular</td><td>deities</td></tr>
<tr><td align="right">deities</td><td>particular deities</td></tr>
<tr><td align="right">particular deities</td><td>surviving</td></tr>
<tr><td align="right">surviving</td><td>on the energy</td></tr>
<tr><td align="right">on the energy</td><td>surviving on the energy</td></tr>
<tr><td align="right">surviving on the energy</td><td>of a given</td></tr>
<tr><td align="right">of a given</td><td>situation</td></tr>
<tr><td align="right">situation</td><td>of a given situation</td></tr>
<tr><td align="right">of a given situation</td><td></td></tr>
</table>

The meeting
of the two
minds
The meeting of the two minds
is the awareness
is the awareness
of the space
they are sharing
together
of the space
they are sharing together

The double-cut
vinyl
umbrella
The double-cut vinyl umbrella
is solid
color
on top
is solid color on top,
your choice
your choice
of aqua,
citron
or fern
of aqua, citron or fern
exteriors
exteriors
and floral
interiors
and floral interiors

the flowing
pattern
the flowing pattern
of all
one's
past
lives
of all one's past lives

The meeting
of the two
minds
The meeting of the two minds
is the awareness
is the awareness
of the space
they are sharing
together
of the space
they are sharing together

The double-cut
vinyl
umbrella
The double-cut vinyl umbrella
is solid
color
on top
is solid color on top,
your choice
your choice
of aqua,
citron
or fern
of aqua, citron or fern
exteriors
exteriors
and floral
interiors
and floral interiors

the flowing
pattern
the flowing pattern
of all
one's
past
lives
of all one's past lives

***from* CANCER IN MY LEFT BALL, 1972**

and the early
part
and the early part
of one's
present
life
of one's present life
right
up
to today
right up to today

They grinned
broadly
They grinned broadly
at each
other
at each other

three
times
three times
three times
green
horses
green horses
came out
of the top
of his head
came out
of the top of his head
green horses came out
of the top of his head
and everyone
in the world
and everyone in the world
heard
their neighing
and everyone in the world
heard their neighing
heard their neighing

and the early
part
and the early part
of one's
present
life
of one's present life
right
up
to today
right up to today

They grinned
broadly
They grinned broadly
at each
other
at each other

three
times
three times
three times
green
horses
green horses
came out
of the top
of his head
came out
of the top of his head
green horses came out
of the top of his head
and everyone
in the world
and everyone in the world
heard
their neighing
and everyone in the world
heard their neighing
heard their neighing

They pulled
each
other
They pulled
each other
closer
They pulled each other closer
closer

When
you look
in this mirror
When you look
in this mirror
it shoots
flames
at you
When you look in this mirror
it shoots flames
at you
it shoots flames at you,
thunderbolts
at you
thunderbolts at you
thunderbolts at you,
it shoots
amrita
it shoots amrita
at you
it shoots amrita at you
at you

Then they squirmed
closer
Then they squirmed closer
Then they squirmed closer

They pulled
each
other
They pulled
each other
closer
They pulled each other closer
closer

When
you look
in this mirror
When you look
in this mirror
it shoots
flames
at you
When you look in this mirror
it shoots flames
at you
it shoots flames at you,
thunderbolts
at you
thunderbolts at you
thunderbolts at you,
it shoots
amrita
it shoots amrita
at you
it shoots amrita at you
at you

Then they squirmed
closer
Then they squirmed closer
Then they squirmed closer

is merely
the opening
up
is merely the opening up
of both
sides
of both sides,
is merely the opening up
of both sides,
opening

get their tremendous
energies
get their tremendous energies
from exploding
stars
from exploding stars
known as
supernovas
known as supernovas
or collapsing
stars
or collapsing stars
known as
pulsars
known as pulsars

they sucked
each
others
they sucked each others
tongues
tongues
they sucked each others tongues
and swapped
spit
and swapped spit
and swapped spit

is merely
the opening
up
is merely the opening up
of both
sides
of both sides,
is merely the opening up
of both sides,
opening
the whole
thing
opening the whole thing
opening the whole thing

stars
from exploding stars
known as
supernovas
known as supernovas
or collapsing
stars
or collapsing stars
known as
pulsars
known as pulsars

they sucked
each
others
they sucked each others
tongues
tongues
they sucked each others tongues
and swapped
spit
and swapped spit
and swapped spit

He was breathing
hard
He was breathing
hard
He was breathing hard
and I felt
his heart
and I felt his heart
pounding
and I felt his heart pounding
pounding
as he leaned
against me
as he leaned against me
as he leaned against me

was able
to ride
was able to ride
the sun's
rays
the sun's rays
was able to ride the sun's rays
wherever
he wished
wherever he wished
wherever he wished

Something
just
opens
Something
just opens
Something just opens,
and there is a kind
of a flash
and there is a kind
of a flash
and there is a kind of a flash,
and that's
all
and that's all
and that's all

He was breathing
hard
He was breathing
hard
He was breathing hard
and I felt
his heart
and I felt his heart
pounding
and I felt his heart pounding
pounding
as he leaned
against me
as he leaned against me
as he leaned against me

was able
to ride
was able to ride
the sun's
rays
the sun's rays
was able to ride the sun's rays
wherever
he wished
wherever he wished
wherever he wished

Something
just
opens
Something
just opens
Something just opens,
and there is a kind
of a flash
and there is a kind
of a flash
and there is a kind of a flash,
and that's
all
and that's all
and that's all

There is
nothing
there
There is nothing
there
There is nothing there

Energy
can only
happen
Energy can only happen
in the absence
of energy
in the absence of energy,
otherwise
there would be
otherwise there would be
just one
big
explosion
just one big explosion

the sword
in his right
hand
the sword in his right hand
and the skull-bowl
of blood
and the skull-bowl of blood
in his left
the sword in his right hand
and the skull-bowl of blood in
his left
in his left

Whatever
happens
Whatever happens,
that's part
of the trip
that's part of the trip

There is
nothing
there
There is nothing
there
There is nothing there

Energy
can only
happen
Energy can only happen
in the absence
of energy
in the absence of energy,
otherwise
there would be
otherwise there would be
just one
big
explosion
just one big explosion

the sword
in his right
hand
the sword in his right hand
and the skull-bowl
of blood
and the skull-bowl of blood
in his left
the sword in his right hand
and the skull-bowl of blood in
his left
in his left

Whatever
happens
Whatever happens,
that's part
of the trip
that's part of the trip

If you
do it
If you do it,
you get
it
you get it
If you do it,
you get it

He is seated
He is seated
on a human
skin
He is seated on a human skin
on a human skin
with hands
and skull
still attached
with hands and skull
still attached
with hands and skull still
attached

we moved
in rhythm
we moved in rhythm
we moved in rhythm,
hips
slamming
against
hips
hips slamming
against hips
hips slamming against hips
as I worked
my body
as I worked my body
in upward
and downward
as I worked my body
in upward and downward
movements
in upward and downward
movements
movements

If you
do it
If you do it,
you get
it
you get it
If you do it,
you get it

He is seated
He is seated
on a human
skin
He is seated on a human skin
on a human skin
with hands
and skull
still attached
with hands and skull
still attached
with hands and skull still
attached

we moved
in rhythm
we moved in rhythm
we moved in rhythm,
hips
slamming
against
hips
hips slamming
against hips
hips slamming against hips
as I worked
my body
as I worked my body
in upward
and downward
as I worked my body
in upward and downward
movements
in upward and downward
movements
movements

was sometimes
able
was sometimes able
to turn
his body
to turn his body
was sometimes able to turn his
body
into a golden
vajra
into a golden vajra
into a golden vajra

It is not
a question
It is not a question
of going
into another
world
of going
of going
into another world
into another world,
this is
another
world
this is another
world
this is another world

and fell
asleep
and fell asleep
in each
others
arms
and fell asleep
in each others arms
in each others arms

was sometimes
able
was sometimes able
to turn
his body
to turn his body
was sometimes able to turn his
body
into a golden
vajra
into a golden vajra
into a golden vajra

It is not
a question
It is not a question
of going
into another
world
of going
of going
into another world
into another world,
this is
another
world
this is another
world
this is another world

and fell
asleep
and fell asleep
in each
others
arms
and fell asleep
in each others arms
in each others arms

access
roads
access roads
that connect
to the east-west
highway
that connect
to the east-west highway
and to the bridge
and to the bridge

the air
around you
the air around you
is liquid
is liquid
and you can feel
the liquid
and you can feel the liquid
being pulled
into your lungs
being pulled into your lungs
as you inhale
as you inhale

One
opens
oneself
completely
One opens
oneself completely
in such a way that
in such a way that,
although
it may only be
for a few
seconds
although it may only be
for a few seconds,
it somehow
means
a great
deal
it somehow means a great deal

two
small
curved
bridges
two small curved bridges
span
the access
roads
span the access roads

the air
around you
the air around you
is liquid
is liquid
and you can feel
the liquid
and you can feel the liquid
being pulled
into your lungs
being pulled into your lungs
as you inhale
as you inhale

One
opens
oneself
completely
One opens
oneself completely
in such a way that
in such a way that,
although
it may only be
for a few
seconds
although it may only be
for a few seconds,
it somehow
means
a great
deal
it somehow means a great deal

Then slowly
release it
Then slowly release it
by exhaling
by exhaling

power
steering
power steering,
four-wheel
drive
four-wheel drive,
an adjustable
seat
an adjustable seat,
a padded
instrument
panel
a padded instrument panel,
as well as
a tinted
windshield
as well as a tinted windshield,
a stereo
tape
deck
a stereo tape deck,
an AM-FM
radio
an AM-FM radio.

Then slowly
release it
Then slowly release it
by exhaling
by exhaling

power
steering
power steering,
four-wheel
drive
four-wheel drive,
an adjustable
seat
an adjustable seat,
a padded
instrument
panel
a padded instrument panel,
as well as
a tinted
windshield
as well as a tinted windshield,
a stereo
tape
deck
a stereo tape deck,
an AM-FM
radio
an AM-FM radio.

(1972)

DAKINI SOFTWARE

When
he was first
When he was first
shot
down
in the back
shot down in the back
When he was first shot down
in the back
he wasn't dead
he wasn't dead
he wasn't dead
so another
guard
came up
so another guard came up
and shot
him
in the head
and shot him in the head
so another guard came up
and shot him in the head

falling
falling
through
a black
hole
through a black hole
falling through a black hole
of our universe
of our universe
of our universe
would come
out
would come out
as antimatter
would come out as antimatter
as antimatter
in the other
universe
in the other universe
in the other universe

When
he was first
When he was first
shot
down
in the back
shot down in the back
When he was first shot down
in the back
he wasn't dead
he wasn't dead
he wasn't dead
so another
guard
came up
so another guard came up
and shot
him
in the head
and shot him in the head
so another guard came up
and shot him in the head

falling
falling
through
a black
hole
through a black hole
falling through a black hole
of our universe
of our universe
of our universe
would come
out
would come out
as antimatter
would come out as antimatter
as antimatter
in the other
universe
in the other universe
in the other universe

from **CANCER IN MY LEFT BALL, 1972**

The mixture
The mixture
spread
into the sink
spread into the sink,
onto
the floor
onto the floor
and under
an electric
water
heater
and under an electric water
heater
and while
the children
were trying
to contain it
and while the children
were trying to contain it,
their father
woke
up
their father woke up

And it's always
different
And it's always different
and always
the same
and always the same,
and it never
stops
and it never stops,
and you go
insane
and you go insane,
and you stay
and you stay
insane
insane

The mixture
The mixture
spread
into the sink
spread into the sink,
onto
the floor
onto the floor
and under
an electric
water
heater
and under an electric water
heater,
and while
the children
were trying
to contain it
and while the children
were trying to contain it,
their father
woke
up
their father woke up

And it's always
different
And it's always different
and always
the same
and always the same,
and it never
stops
and it never stops,
and you go
insane
and you go insane,
and you stay
and you stay
insane
insane

incredible
glittering
incredible glittering
star-spangled
transvestites
star-spangled transvestites
like floats
in the Macy
parade
like floats in the Macy parade

the terrible
couple
the terrible couple
embracing
each
other
embracing each other,
crowned
with skulls
crowned with skulls,
crushing
under their multiple
feet
crushing under their multiple
feet,
both human
beings
both human beings
and animals
and animals

He had no
idea
where
he was
He had no idea
where he was
He had no idea where he was,
but he knew
he wasn't
in the motel
but he knew
he wasn't in the motel
but he knew he wasn't in the
motel

incredible
glittering
incredible glittering
star-spangled
transvestites
star-spangled transvestites
like floats
in the Macy
parade
like floats in the Macy parade

the terrible
couple
the terrible couple
embracing
each
other
embracing each other,
crowned
with skulls
crowned with skulls,
crushing
under their multiple
feet
crushing under their multiple
feet,
both human
beings
both human beings
and animals
and animals

He had no
idea
where
he was
He had no idea
where he was
He had no idea where he was,
but he knew
he wasn't
in the motel
but he knew
he wasn't in the motel
but he knew he wasn't in the
motel

a gradual
dispersion
a gradual dispersion
of the psychic
or mental
atoms
of the psychic or mental atoms
of the dead
person
of the dead person,
directed
by karmic
affinity
directed by karmic affinity,
inevitably
going
to that environment
inevitably going to that
environment
most
congenial
to it
most congenial to it

there
arises
there arises
the longing
for a lasting
world
the longing for a lasting world
the longing for a lasting world
with lasting
pleasures
with lasting pleasures
with lasting pleasures,
and as such
a one
and as such a one
cannot
be found
and as such a one cannot be found
cannot be found

a gradual
dispersion
a gradual dispersion
of the psychic
or mental
atoms
of the psychic or mental atoms
of the dead
person
of the dead person,
directed
by karmic
affinity
directed by karmic affinity,
inevitably
going
to that environment
inevitably going to that
environment
most
congenial
to it
most congenial to it

there
arises
there arises
the longing
for a lasting
world
the longing for a lasting world
the longing for a lasting world
with lasting
pleasures
with lasting pleasures
with lasting pleasures,
and as such
a one
and as such a one
cannot
be found
and as such a one cannot be found
cannot be found

a confused
sensation
a confused sensation
of finding
himself
a confused sensation of finding
himself
on the edge
of a dark
precipice
of finding himself
on the edge of a dark precipice
on the edge of a dark precipice,
on the point
on the point
of casting
himself
over it
of casting himself over it
on the point of casting himself
over it

you can make
your body
you can make your body
so light
you can make your body so light
so light
that it will float
in air
that it will float
that it will float in air
in air

the bodies
the bodies
where
a pea-sized
piece
where a pea-sized piece
would weigh
as much
would weigh as much
as a whole
mountain
as a whole mountain

a confused
sensation
a confused sensation
of finding
himself
a confused sensation of finding
himself
on the edge
of a dark
precipice
of finding himself
on the edge of a dark precipice
on the edge of a dark precipice,
on the point
on the point
of casting
himself
over it
of casting himself over it
on the point of casting himself
over it

you can make
your body
you can make your body
so light
you can make your body so light
so light
that it will float
in air
that it will float
that it will float in air
in air

the bodies
the bodies
where
a pea-sized
piece
where a pea-sized piece
would weigh
as much
would weigh as much
as a whole
mountain
as a whole mountain

Her brocade
dress
Her brocade dress
flashed
with iridescent
hues
flashed with iridescent hues
in the sun
in the sun,
and her jewels
glittered
on her breast
and her jewels glittered on her
breast

The king
asks
him
The king asks him
to marry
his daughter
to marry his daughter
and the moment
he says
'yes'
and the moment
and the moment he says 'yes'
'yes'
the whole
kingdom
disappears
the whole kingdom disappears

felt
the creatures
felt the creatures
they were tearing
to pieces
felt the creatures
they were tearing to pieces
they were tearing to pieces
writhing
under their teeth
writhing under their teeth
writhing under their teeth

Her brocade
dress
Her brocade dress
flashed
with iridescent
hues
flashed with iridescent hues
in the sun
in the sun,
and her jewels
glittered
on her breast
and her jewels glittered on her
breast

The king
asks
him
The king asks him
to marry
his daughter
to marry his daughter
and the moment
he says
'yes'
and the moment
and the moment he says 'yes'
'yes'
the whole
kingdom
disappears
the whole kingdom disappears

felt
the creatures
felt the creatures
they were tearing
to pieces
felt the creatures
they were tearing to pieces
they were tearing to pieces
writhing
under their teeth
writhing under their teeth
writhing under their teeth

the Red
Dakini
the Red Dakini
holding
a crescent
knife
the Red Dakini holding a
crescent knife
holding a crescent knife
and a skull
filled
with blood
and a skull
and a skull
filled with blood
filled with blood

Clouds
of gas
Clouds of gas,
ten thousand
times
the weight
of the sun
ten thousand times
the weight of the sun,
laced
with bright
flashes
laced with bright flashes
of electricity
of electricity,
gently
waft
through
space
gently waft through space

the Red
Dakini
the Red Dakini
holding
a crescent
knife
the Red Dakini holding a
crescent knife
holding a crescent knife
and a skull
filled
with blood
and a skull
and a skull
filled with blood
filled with blood

Clouds
of gas
Clouds of gas,
ten thousand
times
the weight
of the sun
ten thousand times
the weight of the sun,
laced
with bright
flashes
laced with bright flashes
of electricity
of electricity,
gently
waft
through
space
gently waft through space

I want
to come
I want to come
with you
I want to come with you
with you

All
the while
All the while
he cries
out
All the while he cries out
with a tense,
high-pitched
shriek
he cries out with a tense,
high-pitched shriek
with a tense, high-pitched shriek

Hopelessness
Hopelessness
that comes
with the realization
that comes with the realization
that you can't
commit
suicide
that you can't commit suicide
that you can't
end it
that you can't end it

We tore
up and down
the streets
We tore up and down the streets
flinging
empty
bottles
flinging empty bottles
into plate
glass
windows
into plate glass windows

I want
to come
I want to come
with you
I want to come with you
with you

All
the while
All the while
he cries
out
All the while he cries out
with a tense,
high-pitched
shriek
he cries out with a tense,
high-pitched shriek
with a tense, high-pitched shriek

Hopelessness
Hopelessness
that comes
with the realization
that comes with the realization
that you can't
commit
suicide
that you can't commit suicide
that you can't
end it
that you can't end it

We tore
up and down
the streets
We tore up and down the streets
flinging
empty
bottles
flinging empty bottles
into plate
glass
windows
into plate glass windows

near-nude
girls
near-nude girls
with neon
eyelids
with neon eyelids
and black
vampire
lipstick
and black vampire lipstick

he could not
imagine
himself
he could not imagine himself
otherwise
otherwise
he could not imagine himself
otherwise

And then I heard
And then I heard
the sound
of another
motor
the sound of another motor
rushing
at me
rushing at me

near-nude
girls
near-nude girls
with neon
eyelids
with neon eyelids
and black
vampire
lipstick
and black vampire lipstick

he could not
imagine
himself
he could not imagine himself
otherwise
otherwise
he could not imagine himself
otherwise

And then I heard
And then I heard
the sound
of another
motor
the sound of another motor
rushing
at me
rushing at me

The Guava
bomb
The Guava bomb
can explode
on impact
can explode on impact,
in the air
in the air,
or with a time
delay
fuse
or with a time delay fuse,
spewing
400,000
to 500,000
ball-bearing
pellets
spewing 400,000 to 500,000
ball-bearing pellets
in a 360 degree
pattern
in a 360 degree pattern,
and are designed
for use
against
and are designed for use against
unprotected
human
flesh
unprotected human flesh

The Guava
bomb
The Guava bomb
can explode
on impact
can explode on impact,
in the air
in the air,
or with a time
delay
fuse
or with a time delay fuse,
spewing
400,000
to 500,000
ball-bearing
pellets
spewing 400,000 to 500,000
ball-bearing pellets
in a 360 degree
pattern
in a 360 degree pattern,
and are designed
for use
against
and are designed for use against
unprotected
human
flesh
unprotected human flesh

The body
The body
is violently
torn
apart
The body is violently
torn apart
is violently torn apart
into molecules
into molecules
into molecules

drums
and thigh-bone
trumpets
drums and thigh-bone trumpets,
skull-timbrels
skull-timbrels,
banners
of gigantic
human
hides
banners of gigantic human
hides,
human-hide
canopies
human-hide canopies,
human-hide
bannerettes
human-hide bannerettes,
fumes
of human-fat
incense
fumes of human-fat incense

he did not really
know
he did not really know
whether
he was awake
whether he was awake
or asleep
or asleep

The body
The body
is violently
torn
apart
The body is violently
torn apart
is violently torn apart
into molecules
into molecules
into molecules

drums
and thigh-bone
trumpets
drums and thigh-bone trumpets,
skull-timbrels
skull-timbrels,
banners
of gigantic
human
hides
banners of gigantic human
hides,
human-hide
canopies
human-hide canopies,
human-hide
bannerettes
human-hide bannerettes,
fumes
of human-fat
incense
fumes of human-fat incense

he did not really
know
he did not really know
whether
he was awake
whether he was awake
or asleep
or asleep

A car
passed
A car passed
and I tried
to cry out
and I tried to cry out
A car passed and I tried to cry
out
but it was useless
but it was useless
but it was useless

an obese
Medusa
an obese Medusa
with life-like
rubber
snakes
with life-like rubber snakes
writhing
in her hair
writhing in her hair

through which
matter
through which matter
from other
universes
from other universes,
existing
existing
in other
space-time
reference
frames
in other space-time reference
frames,
is entering
our universe
is entering our universe

A car
passed
A car passed
and I tried
to cry out
and I tried to cry out
A car passed and I tried to cry
out
but it was useless
but it was useless
but it was useless

an obese
Medusa
an obese Medusa
with life-like
rubber
snakes
with life-like rubber snakes
writhing
in her hair
writhing in her hair

through which
matter
through which matter
from other
universes
from other universes,
existing
existing
in other
space-time
reference
frames
in other space-time reference
frames,
is entering
our universe
is entering our universe

we cannot
desire
we cannot desire
the one
the one
without
inviting
the other
without inviting the other

I don't
think
I don't think
I will sing
I will sing
any more
just
now
I don't think I will sing
any more
just now
any more just now;
or ever
or ever
or ever

He is extremely
short
He is extremely short
with stumpy
legs
with stumpy legs,
a bulging
belly
a bulging belly,
protruding
eyes
protruding eyes
and a handlebar
mustache
and a handlebar mustache

we cannot
desire
we cannot desire
the one
the one
without
inviting
the other
without inviting the other

I don't
think
I don't think
I will sing
I will sing
any more
just
now
I don't think I will sing
any more
just now
any more just now;
or ever
or ever
or ever

He is extremely
short
He is extremely short
with stumpy
legs
with stumpy legs,
a bulging
belly
a bulging belly,
protruding
eyes
protruding eyes
and a handlebar
mustache
and a handlebar mustache

conditions
a continuous
process
conditions a continuous process
of becoming
of becoming
in the direction
of the desired
forms
in the direction of the desired
forms

As one
of them
As one of them
stopped
stopped
urinating
on me
stopped urinating on me
urinating on me
another
moved in
another moved in
and took
his place
another moved in and took his
place
and took his place

"go
down
the drain
go down
the drain
go down the drain"
into a black
hole
into a black hole
into a black hole,
vanishing
entirely
vanishing entirely
from our universe
vanishing entirely from our
universe
from our universe

conditions
a continuous
process
conditions a continuous process
of becoming
of becoming
in the direction
of the desired
forms
in the direction of the desired
forms

As one
of them
As one of them
stopped
stopped
urinating
on me
stopped urinating on me
urinating on me
another
moved in
another moved in
and took
his place
another moved in and took his
place
and took his place

"go
down
the drain
go down
the drain
go down the drain"
into a black
hole
into a black hole
into a black hole,
vanishing
entirely
vanishing entirely
from our universe
vanishing entirely from our
universe
from our universe

Our having had
this opportunity
Our having had this opportunity
to be
together
to be together
is the beginning
of a union
is the beginning of a union
that will last
for many
lives
that will last for many lives

He sucks
constantly
He sucks constantly
as if hungry
as if hungry,
yet he will not
eat
yet he will not eat
and if he does
and if he does,
he vomits
he vomits

are then spewed
out
are then spewed out
into space
are then spewed out into space
into space
to become parts
of other
stars
and planets
to become parts of other stars
and planets

Our having had
this opportunity
Our having had this opportunity
to be
together
to be together
is the beginning
of a union
is the beginning of a union
that will last
for many
lives
that will last for many lives

He sucks
constantly
He sucks constantly
as if hungry
as if hungry,
yet he will not
eat
yet he will not eat
and if he does
and if he does,
he vomits
he vomits

are then spewed
out
are then spewed out
into space
are then spewed out into space
into space
to become parts
of other
stars
and planets
to become parts of other stars
and planets

All
the king’s
All the king’s
horses
All the king’s horses,
all
the king’s
all the king’s
men
all the king’s men,
couldn’t put
couldn’t put
our two
hearts
together
again
our two hearts
our two hearts together again
together again

So that the loss
So that the loss
was even more
utterly
felt
was even more utterly felt
So that the loss
was even more utterly felt,
as a kind
of permanent
doom
as a kind
of permanent doom
of my desires
of my desires
as a kind of permanent doom
of my desires
as I knew
them
as I knew them
since childhood
as I knew them since childhood
since childhood

All
the king’s
All the king’s
horses
All the king’s horses,
all
the king’s
all the king’s
men
all the king’s men,
couldn’t put
couldn’t put
our two
hearts
together
again
our two hearts
our two hearts together again
together again

So that the loss
So that the loss
was even more
utterly
felt
was even more utterly felt
So that the loss
was even more utterly felt,
as a kind
of permanent
doom
as a kind
of permanent doom
of my desires
of my desires
as a kind of permanent doom
of my desires
as I knew
them
as I knew them
since childhood
as I knew them since childhood
since childhood

Do not try
to dispel
this fear
Do not try to dispel this fear,
but dwell
on it
but dwell on it
clearly
and loosely
clearly and loosely

It is like
the person
It is like the person
who does not
worry
who does not worry
about
thieves
about thieves
because
he has nothing
that thieves
can take
away
because he has nothing
that thieves can take away

A dozen
people
A dozen people,
calmly
looted
calmly looted
a rice
store
a rice store
shoveling
the grains
into sacks
and boxes
shoveling the grains
into sacks and boxes

Do not try
to dispel
this fear
Do not try to dispel this fear,
but dwell
on it
but dwell on it
clearly
and loosely
clearly and loosely

It is like
the person
It is like the person
who does not
worry
who does not worry
about
thieves
about thieves
because
he has nothing
that thieves
can take
away
because he has nothing
that thieves can take away

A dozen
people
A dozen people,
calmly
looted
calmly looted
a rice
store
a rice store
shoveling
the grains
into sacks
and boxes
shoveling the grains
into sacks and boxes

***from* CANCER IN MY LEFT BALL, 1972**

vanishing
vanishing
in a black
hole
in a black hole
in our universe
vanishing in a black hole
in our universe
in our universe
is flowing
is flowing
into the other
universe
into the other universe
is flowing into the other universe

The symbols
The symbols
that can be seen
in daily
events
that can be seen in daily events
is the language
of the dakinis
is the language of the dakinis

The main
entrance
lobby
The main entrance lobby
leads
to a concourse
leads to a concourse
that runs
completely
around
the building
that runs completely
around the building

vanishing
vanishing
in a black
hole
in a black hole
in our universe
vanishing in a black hole
in our universe
in our universe
is flowing
is flowing
into the other
universe
into the other universe
is flowing into the other universe

The symbols
The symbols
that can be seen
in daily
events
that can be seen in daily events
is the language
of the dakinis
is the language of the dakinis

The main
entrance
lobby
The main entrance lobby
leads
to a concourse
leads to a concourse
that runs
completely
around
the building
that runs completely
around the building

I am
nowhere
I am nowhere
anything
to anyone
anything to anyone
I am nowhere anything to
anyone,
and nowhere
and nowhere
is there
anyone
is there anyone
and nowhere is there anyone
who can be
anything
who can be anything
to me
who can be anything to me
to me

compressed
compressed
into one
infinitesimally
tiny
compressed
into one infinitesimally tiny,
invisible
point
invisible point
in space
invisible point in space
in space

filling
with music
filling with music
the whole
world-systems
the whole world-systems
and causing
them
to vibrate
and causing them
to vibrate

I am
nowhere
I am nowhere
anything
to anyone
anything to anyone
I am nowhere anything to
anyone,
and nowhere
and nowhere
is there
anyone
is there anyone
and nowhere is there anyone
who can be
anything
who can be anything
to me
who can be anything to me
to me

compressed
compressed
into one
infinitesimally
tiny
compressed
into one infinitesimally tiny,
invisible
point
invisible point
in space
invisible point in space
in space

filling
with music
filling with music
the whole
world-systems
the whole world-systems
and causing
them
to vibrate
and causing them
to vibrate

and causing them to vibrate,
to quake
and tremble
to quake and tremble
to quake and tremble

Sitting
Sitting
with crossed
legs
Sitting with crossed legs
with crossed legs,
his feet
resting
on his thighs
his feet
resting on his thighs
his feet resting on his thighs,
his head
and body
his head and body
upright
and rigid
upright and rigid
his head and body
upright and rigid,
motionless
motionless
motionless

I would
not say
I would not say
that samsara
does not
exist
I would not say
that samsara does not exist
that samsara does not exist,
but that it is
not
real
but that it is not
real
but that it is not real

and causing them to vibrate,
to quake
and tremble
to quake and tremble
to quake and tremble

Sitting
Sitting
with crossed
legs
Sitting with crossed legs
with crossed legs,
his feet
resting
on his thighs
his feet
resting on his thighs
his feet resting on his thighs,
his head
and body
his head and body
upright
and rigid
upright and rigid
his head and body
upright and rigid,
motionless
motionless
motionless

I would
not say
I would not say
that samsara
does not
exist
I would not say
that samsara does not exist
that samsara does not exist,
but that it is
not
real
but that it is not
real
but that it is not real

phenomenal
amounts
phenomenal amounts
of energy
of energy
phenomenal amounts of energy
are being
given
off
are being given off
by something
that cannot
be seen
by something that cannot be seen
are being given off
by something that cannot be seen

I have
forgotten
I have forgotten
it all
I have forgotten it all
it all,
and anyway
and anyway
and anyway
there is
nothing
to remember
there is nothing
to remember
there is nothing to remember

he felt
himself
he felt himself
floating
he felt himself floating
floating
on a calm
sea
on a calm sea
of luminous
whiteness
on a calm sea of luminous
whiteness
of luminous whiteness

phenomenal
amounts
phenomenal amounts
of energy
of energy
phenomenal amounts of energy
are being
given
off
are being given off
by something
that cannot
be seen
by something that cannot be seen
are being given off
by something that cannot be seen

I have
forgotten
I have forgotten
it all
I have forgotten it all
it all,
and anyway
and anyway
and anyway
there is
nothing
to remember
there is nothing
to remember
there is nothing to remember

he felt
himself
he felt himself
floating
he felt himself floating
floating
on a calm
sea
on a calm sea
of luminous
whiteness
on a calm sea of luminous
whiteness
of luminous whiteness

from **CANCER IN MY LEFT BALL, 1972**

I am sure
I am sure
that this
that this
is not
the end
I am sure
that this is not the end
is not the end

relating
relating
to the luminous
character
of all
our experiences
the luminous character
of all our experiences
of all our experiences,
or the primordial
radiance
or the primordial radiance
or the primordial radiance,
light
which in the narrower
sense
of the word
light
light
which in the narrower sense
of the word
is our actual
experience
is our actual experience
of daily
life
is our actual experience of daily
life
of daily life

A beer
can
A beer can
was shoved
into my hand
was shoved into my hand
and I started
to drink
and I started to drink

I am sure
I am sure
that this
that this
is not
the end
I am sure
that this is not the end
is not the end

relating
relating
to the luminous
character
of all
our experiences
the luminous character
of all our experiences
of all our experiences,
or the primordial
radiance
or the primordial radiance
or the primordial radiance,
light
which in the narrower
sense
of the word
light
light
which in the narrower sense
of the word
is our actual
experience
is our actual experience
of daily
life
is our actual experience of daily
life
of daily life

A beer
can
A beer can
was shoved
into my hand
was shoved into my hand
and I started
to drink
and I started to drink

cosmic
suffering
cosmic suffering
cosmic suffering,
the suffering
implicit
in the cosmic
law
the suffering implicit
in the cosmic law,
which chains us
to our deeds
which chains us to our deeds,
good
as well as
bad
good as well as bad,
which chains us to our deeds,
good as well as bad,
and drives us
incessantly
and drives us incessantly
round
and drives us incessantly round
round
in a restless
circle
in a restless circle
from form
to form
from form to form
in a restless circle
from form to form

When
I woke up
again
When I woke up
again
When I woke up again
I was alone
I was alone
I was alone

cosmic
suffering
cosmic suffering
cosmic suffering,
the suffering
implicit
in the cosmic
law
the suffering implicit
in the cosmic law,
which chains us
to our deeds
which chains us to our deeds,
good
as well as
bad
good as well as bad,
which chains us to our deeds,
good as well as bad,
and drives us
incessantly
and drives us incessantly
round
and drives us incessantly round
round
in a restless
circle
in a restless circle
from form
to form
from form to form
in a restless circle
from form to form

When
I woke up
again
When I woke up
again
When I woke up again
I was alone
I was alone
I was alone

Buddhas
are colonels
Buddhas are colonels
who shout
at trainees
Buddhas are colonels
who shout
who shout at trainees
at trainees,
"If you can't
strangle
a chicken
If you can't strangle
a chicken
If you can't strangle a chicken,
how
can you ever
make love
to a woman
how can you ever
make love to a woman
how can you ever make love to a
woman?"

Buddha
is Mr. Leon
Buddha is Mr. Leon
grabbing
a heavy
butcher
knife
Buddha is Mr. Leon
grabbing
a heavy butcher knife
grabbing a heavy butcher knife
and throwing it
and throwing it
at the gunman
and throwing it at the gunman
at the gunman,
who shoots
Mr. Leon
in the right
thigh
who shoots Mr. Leon
in the right thigh
who shoots Mr. Leon in the
right thigh,

Buddhas
are colonels
Buddhas are colonels
who shout
at trainees
Buddhas are colonels
who shout
who shout at trainees
at trainees,
"If you can't
strangle
a chicken
If you can't strangle
a chicken
If you can't strangle a chicken,
how
can you ever
make love
to a woman
how can you ever
make love to a woman
how can you ever make love to a
woman?"

Buddha
is Mr. Leon
Buddha is Mr. Leon
grabbing
a heavy
butcher
knife
Buddha is Mr. Leon
grabbing
a heavy butcher knife
grabbing a heavy butcher knife
and throwing it
and throwing it
at the gunman
and throwing it at the gunman
at the gunman,
who shoots
Mr. Leon
in the right
thigh
who shoots Mr. Leon
in the right thigh
who shoots Mr. Leon in the
right thigh,
and both men

and both men
fleeing
and both men fleeing
without
taking
any money
and both men fleeing
without taking
any money
without taking any money

Buddhas
are itinerant
street
vendors
Buddhas
Buddhas are itinerant street
vendors
are itinerant street vendors
who seem
to come
out
of nowhere
who seem to come out
of nowhere
with their folding
tables
and well-worn
cartons
who seem to come out of
nowhere
with their folding tables
and well-worn cartons
from which they sell
umbrellas
from which they sell umbrellas,
neckties
neckties,
handbags
handbags,
costume
jewelry
costume jewelry,
mechanical
toys
mechanical toys,
pretzels
pretzels,
and a variety

fleeing
and both men fleeing
without
taking
any money
and both men fleeing
without taking
any money
without taking any money

Buddhas
are itinerant
street
vendors
Buddhas
Buddhas are itinerant street
vendors
are itinerant street vendors
who seem
to come
out
of nowhere
who seem to come out
of nowhere
with their folding
tables
and well-worn
cartons
who seem to come out of
nowhere
with their folding tables
and well-worn cartons
from which they sell
umbrellas
from which they sell umbrellas,
neckties
neckties,
handbags
handbags,
costume
jewelry
costume jewelry,
mechanical
toys
mechanical toys,
pretzels
pretzels,
and a variety
of other

of other
merchandise
and a variety of other
merchandise

Buddhas
are species
Buddhas are species
in which technology
has gone
out of control
in which technology
has gone out of control
in which technology has gone
out of control,
a technological
cancer
a technological cancer
spreading
through
our galaxy
spreading through our galaxy
a technological cancer
spreading through our galaxy

Buddha
Buddha
is like the most beautiful
diamond
Buddha is like the most beautiful
diamond
is like the most beautiful
diamond
hidden
hidden
hidden in the mouth
of a corpse
in the mouth
of a corpse
in the mouth of a corpse

merchandise
and a variety of other
merchandise

Buddhas
are species
Buddhas are species
in which technology
has gone
out of control
in which technology
has gone out of control
in which technology has gone
out of control,
a technological
cancer
a technological cancer
spreading
through
our galaxy
spreading through our galaxy
a technological cancer
spreading through our galaxy

Buddha
Buddha
is like the most beautiful
diamond
Buddha is like the most beautiful
diamond
is like the most beautiful
diamond
hidden
hidden
hidden in the mouth
of a corpse
in the mouth
of a corpse
in the mouth of a corpse

Buddha
is an ordinary
star
Buddha is an ordinary star
and a pulsar
Buddha is an ordinary star and
a pulsar
and a pulsar,
or pulsing
object
or pulsing object
of extreme
density
or pulsing object of extreme
density
of extreme density,
waltzing
together
waltzing together
through space
waltzing together through space
far out
in the constellation
Hercules
through space far out
in the constellation Hercules
far out in the constellation
Hercules

Buddha
is an ordinary
star
Buddha is an ordinary star
and a pulsar
Buddha is an ordinary star and
a pulsar
and a pulsar,
or pulsing
object
or pulsing object
of extreme
density
or pulsing object of extreme
density
of extreme density,
waltzing
together
waltzing together
through space
waltzing together through space
far out
in the constellation
Hercules
through space far out
in the constellation Hercules
far out in the constellation
Hercules

Buddha
is this mind
Buddha is this mind
and its quality
of creating
differences
Buddha is this mind
and its quality
of creating differences
and its quality of creating
differences,
that is not only
illusory
that is not only illusory
that is not only illusory,
but in fact
but in fact
does not
exist
does not exist
and has never been
born
but in fact does not exist
and has never been born
and has never been born

Buddha
is this mind
Buddha is this mind
and its quality
of creating
differences
Buddha is this mind
and its quality
of creating differences
and its quality of creating
differences,
that is not only
illusory
that is not only illusory
that is not only illusory,
but in fact
but in fact
does not
exist
does not exist
and has never been
born
but in fact does not exist
and has never been born
and has never been born

(1971)

SUICIDE SUTRA

Everyone is invited to participate in this poem. This is an audience participation poem. Please follow the instructions as you read them, and tighten the muscles of your body. Tighten each individual muscle and hold it. You should become uptight.

You can't
remember
where you
are,
you have forgotten
who you are,
you can't even
remember
what the words
mean,
and you want
to change it
and you want to change it
and you want to change it,
and you don't
know how
to do it.

Tighten
your fingers,
tighten
your hands,
tighten
your wrists,
tighten
your forearms

and your elbows,
tighten
your upper arms
and tighten
your shoulders.

You are
in jail
you are in jail
you are in jail,
you are locked
in this space,
it is dark
and smelly,
and filthy,
completely
depressing
completely depressing.

You are
alone
you are alone,
and you are
lonely
and you are lonely
and you are lonely,
and it's eating
your heart
out,
and there's
no way
out.

Tighten
your shoulders,

tighten
your back muscles,
tighten
the curve
in your back,
and tighten
the cheeks
of your ass.

The air
is liquid
the air is liquid,
thick
and heavy
pressing
in
on you.

Giant
boulders
are crushing
against
each other,
giant boulders
are crushing you,
and they are crushing you,
and they are
killing you
and they are killing you.
The air
around
your body
turns
to solid
rock,

and it's smothering
you
and it's smothering you
and it's smothering you,
and you can feel it
inside your chest
breaking your chest
breaking
your heart.

Tighten
your chest
muscles,
tighten
your stomach
muscles,
tighten
your gut,
tighten the cheeks
of your ass,
your rib
cage
is locked.

You are
angry
you are angry
you are angry,
and you really
hate it
and you really hate it
and you really hate it,
and you want
to scream

and you want to scream,
but you can't
but you can't
because
the sound
is locked
in your throat
the sound is
locked in your throat.

They are pulling
your arms
off
they are pulling your arms off,
they are ripping
your arms off
your body,
they are twisting
your head
off
they are twisting your head off.

Tighten
your neck,
tighten
your forehead,
tighten
your nose,
tighten
your lips,
tighten
your cheeks,
tighten
your jaw,

tighten
the skin
on your skull.

Your eyes
are open
your eyes are open,
and your eyes
are popping
out
of your head
and your eyes are popping
out of your head.

You are in a doorless
burning
house
you are in a doorless burning house,
enclosed
enclosed
enclosed inside
another
doorless
burning
house
inside another doorless burning house,
inside
another
inside another,
and you are crying
and you are crying
and you are crying.

Tighten
your shoulders,

tighten
your arms,
tighten
your wrists,
tighten
your hand,
tighten
your fingers.

There is
a gun
in your hand
there is a gun in your hand,
a 38-caliber
revolver,
and it's pointing
at your face
and it's pointing at your face
and it's pointing at your face,
and you pull
the trigger
and you pull
and you pull the trigger,
the bullet
shoots
slowly
the bullet shoots slowly
toward
your head
shoots slowly toward your head,
you are committing
suicide
you are committing suicide
you are committing suicide,
and it smashes

into your face
and it smashes into your face
and it smashes into your face,
and blows
your skull
open
and blows your skull open,
blood
and brains
and flesh
and skin
and hair
fly
into the air.

You are dying
you are dying
you are dying
you are dying,
and you're still
trying
to hold it
together,
trying
to hold
it in,
trying to hold
the bloody
mess
as it scatters
in the room.

Tighten
your shoulders,
straighten

your back,
suck in
your crotch
and your asshole,
tighten
your gut.

You are dead
you are dead
you are dead
you are dead,
and it's the same
and it's the same
and it's the same,
nothing
has changed
nothing
nothing
nothing has changed,
only it's a little
worse,
it's more
horrible
it's more horrible,
you're just
in another
hell,
and there's
no way
out
and there's no
way out
and there's no way out.

There's nothing
else
to do,
but tighten
your thigh
muscles,
and tighten
your knees,
tighten
your calves,
tighten
your ankles,
tighten
your feet,
and tighten
your toes.

There is
no time
off,
and if you go
to sleep
you blow it,
you are totally
lost
you are totally lost
and you have forgotten
you are dead
and you have forgotten you are dead.

Go over
your body
and tighten
the muscles
that have loosened,
every muscle

must be totally
intensified,
you are hard
as a rock.

You hear
the long
low
roar
of a jet
plane
you hear the long low roar
of a jet plane,
and it gets
louder
and louder
and it gets louder
and louder
and it gets louder and louder
into a piercing
shriek
overhead.

A napalm
bomb
explodes
napalm
napalm
napalm
sliding
everywhere
sliding everywhere,
and you are covered
with burning
napalm

and you are covered
with burning napalm
for an instant
you can't believe
it's really happening.

Your skin
is burning
your skin is burning
your skin is burning,
every inch of you
is burning,
napalm
that sticks
and can't be
rubbed off
or put out,
and has to burn out.

Your skin
is blistering
your skin is blistering,
and there are blisters
inside
those blisters
and there are blisters
inside those blisters,
and cracking blisters
inside those,
and more
inside those
and more inside those.

Your muscles
are cooking,

you smell
like a juicy
steak
barbecuing
on a charcoal
grill.

Your eyes
are open
and your eyes
are popping out
of your head,
and your eyes
are burning
and your eyes are burning,
and you have to get
out of here.

You lean
forward
on your left
leg,
lean gently
forward,
and suck in
your asshole,
and suck in
your crotch,
and straighten
your back.

Feel
the energy
inside
your gut

running
up
your spine,
flowing
in a white
channel
up into
your head,
and you go
slowly
and you go slowly
up
and up
and up
and up,
it's like you're
a baby
being born
from your mother,
it's like being
squeezed
through
a steel net,
and you go
higher
and you go higher,
and higher
and higher
and higher.

It's like being
born,
a flower
opening,
and it is effortless

and it is effortless
and it is effortless,
and becomes
cooler
and cooler
and cooler,
and calm
and calm
and calm.

You haven't gotten
anywhere,
only
here.

(1973)

from SUBDUING DEMONS IN AMERICA

and you are
floating
on a river
and you are floating
on a river
and you are floating on a river,
floating
down
the Green
River
floating down
the Green River
floating down the Green River
in Utah
in Utah
in Utah,
floating
on a rubber
raft
floating on a rubber raft
for 7 days
for 7 days
floating on a rubber raft for 7
days,
just lying
there
on this water
bed
just lying there on this water bed,
floating
through
the canyons
floating
through the canyons

and you are
floating
on a river
and you are floating
on a river
and you are floating on a river,
floating
down
the Green
River
floating down
the Green River
floating down the Green River
in Utah
in Utah
in Utah,
floating
on a rubber
raft
floating on a rubber raft
for 7 days
for 7 days
floating on a rubber raft for 7
days,
just lying
there
on this water
bed
just lying there on this water bed,
floating
through
the canyons
floating
through the canyons
floating through the canyons,

floating through the canyons,
and you become
part
of the river
and you become part
of the river
and you become part of the river,
and the canyon
walls
are 2000
feet
high
and the canyon walls
and the canyon walls are 2000 feet
high
are 2000 feet high
on either
side
of you
on either side of you,
and you see
clearly
and continuously
and you see clearly
and continuously
250 million
years
in giant
layers
of rock
250 million years
in giant layers of rock,
and there are
castles
and palaces
and there are castles
and palaces
and there are castles and palaces,
and the canyon
walls
are Persepolis
and Susa
and the canyon walls
are Persepolis and Susa

and you become
part
of the river
and you become part
of the river
and you become part of the river,
and the canyon
walls
are 2000
feet
high
and the canyon walls
and the canyon walls are 2000 feet
high
are 2000 feet high
on either
side
of you
on either side of you,
and you see
clearly
and continuously
and you see clearly
and continuously
250 million
years
in giant
layers
of rock
250 million years
in giant layers of rock,
and there are
castles
and palaces
and there are castles
and palaces
and there are castles and palaces,
and the canyon
walls
are Persepolis
and Susa
and the canyon walls
are Persepolis and Susa
are Persepolis and Susa

are Persepolis and Susa
and Darius
and Darius
and Syrian
slaves
carrying
offerings
and Syrian slaves carrying offerings,
and the houses
of gods
and the houses of gods,
and the temples
of gods
and the temples of gods,
endless
gods
endless gods
endless gods,
and jealous
gods
and jealous gods
and jealous gods
in endless
worlds
in endless worlds
in endless worlds

it is fascinating
and spectacular
it is fascinating and spectacular
it is fascinating and spectacular,
the rocks
are enchanting
the rocks are enchanting
the rocks are enchanting,
your mind
keeps
looking
at the rocks
your mind keeps looking
at the rocks

and Darius
and Darius
and Syrian
slaves
carrying
offerings
and Syrian slaves carrying offerings,
and the houses
of gods
and the houses of gods,
and the temples
of gods
and the temples of gods,
endless
gods
endless gods
endless gods,
and jealous
gods
and jealous gods
and jealous gods
in endless
worlds
in endless worlds
in endless worlds

it is fascinating
and spectacular
it is fascinating and spectacular
it is fascinating and spectacular,
the rocks
are enchanting
the rocks are enchanting
the rocks are enchanting,
your mind
keeps
looking
at the rocks
your mind keeps looking
at the rocks
your mind keeps looking at the rocks,

your mind keeps looking at the rocks,
looking
for something
and not
finding it
looking for something
and not finding it
looking for something and not finding it,
because you have
forgotten
you are
water
because you have forgotten
you are water
because you have forgotten you are
water,
the heavy
water
the heavy water
flowing
the heavy water flowing
forward
flowing forward
forward,
on
and on
on and on
on and on,
and down
and down
and down,
and Green
and Green
and Green,
without
ever
thinking
of being water
without ever thinking
of being water
without ever thinking of being water,
and it's totally
empty
and it's totally empty

looking
for something
and not
finding it
looking for something
and not finding it
looking for something and not finding it,
because you have
forgotten
you are
water
because you have forgotten
you are water
because you have forgotten you are
water,
the heavy
water
the heavy water
flowing
the heavy water flowing
forward
flowing forward
forward,
on
and on
on and on
on and on,
and down
and down
and down,
and Green
and Green
and Green,
without
ever
thinking
of being water
without ever thinking
of being water
without ever thinking of being water,
and it's totally
empty
and it's totally empty
and it's totally empty,

and it's totally empty,
flowing
like this room
is flowing
flowing like this room
is flowing
flowing like this room is flowing,
heavy
and empty
and boring
heavy and empty and boring
heavy and empty and boring as
this room
as this room,
the same
as the space
you're in
now
the same as the space
you're in now
the same as the space you're in
now

and in honor
of the day
and in honor of the day
and in honor of the day,
he shed
his paratrooper
uniform
he shed his paratrooper uniform
and beret
he shed his paratrooper uniform
and beret,
for an elegant
white
and gold
robe
for an elegant
white and gold robe
and cap
for an elegant white and gold
robe
and cap

flowing
like this room
is flowing
flowing like this room
is flowing
flowing like this room is flowing,
heavy
and empty
and boring
heavy and empty and boring
heavy and empty and boring as
this room
as this room,
the same
as the space
you're in
now
the same as the space
you're in now
the same as the space you're in
now

and in honor
of the day
and in honor of the day
and in honor of the day,
he shed
his paratrooper
uniform
he shed his paratrooper uniform
and beret
he shed his paratrooper uniform
and beret,
for an elegant
white
and gold
robe
for an elegant
white and gold robe
and cap
for an elegant white and gold
robe
and cap

and it's prime
ribs
of beef
and it's prime
ribs of beef
and it's prime ribs of beef
and fresh
stone
crab
and fresh
stone crab
and fresh stone crab
and big
black
mushrooms
sauteed
in butter
and big
black mushrooms
and big black mushrooms
sauteed in butter,
and champagne
and champagne
and champagne
and cognac
and cognac
and cognac,
and it feels
so good
and it feels so good
and it feels so good,
you've forgotten
you've forgotten
how
it feels
you've forgotten how it feels
how it feels,
and it's never
going
to end

and it's prime
ribs
of beef
and it's prime
ribs of beef
and it's prime ribs of beef
and fresh
stone
crab
and fresh
stone crab
and fresh stone crab
and big
black
mushrooms
sauteed
in butter
and big
black mushrooms
and big black mushrooms
sauteed in butter,
and champagne
and champagne
and champagne
and cognac
and cognac
and cognac,
and it feels
so good
and it feels so good
and it feels so good,
you've forgotten
you've forgotten
how
it feels
you've forgotten how it feels
how it feels,
and it's never
going
to end
and it's never going to end

and it's never going to end
because
it belongs
to you
and it's never going to end
because it belongs
to you
because it belongs to you,
and it's milk
and honey
and it's milk and honey
and it's milk and honey,
and kisses
and tongues
and kisses and tongues
and kisses and tongues,
and touchies
and feelies
and touchies and feelies
and touchies and feelies,
and Philadelphia
cream
cheese
and Philadelphia
cream cheese
and Philadelphia cream cheese,
and it's sweet
warm
flesh
and it's sweet
warm flesh
and it's sweet warm flesh,
and great
big
hugs
and great big
hugs
and great big hugs,
and lots
of cums
and lots of cums
and lots of cums,

because
it belongs
to you
and it's never going to end
because it belongs
to you
because it belongs to you,
and it's milk
and honey
and it's milk and honey
and it's milk and honey,
and kisses
and tongues
and kisses and tongues
and kisses and tongues,
and touchies
and feelies
and touchies and feelies
and touchies and feelies,
and Philadelphia
cream
cheese
and Philadelphia
cream cheese
and Philadelphia cream cheese,
and it's sweet
warm
flesh
and it's sweet
warm flesh
and it's sweet warm flesh,
and great
big
hugs
and great big
hugs
and great big hugs,
and lots
of cums
and lots of cums
and lots of cums,

and the juicy
Georgia
peach
and the juicy
Georgia peach
and the juicy Georgia peach
is getting
a little
overripe
is getting a little
overripe
and a slight
feeling
of insecurity
is getting a little overripe,
and a slight feeling
of insecurity
and a slight feeling of insecurity,
that gradually
begins
to spiral
that gradually begins
to spiral
that gradually begins to spiral,
and the plug
in the bathtub
and the plug in the bathtub
gets pulled
gets pulled
and the plug in the bathtub gets
pulled,
and everything
goes down
the drain
and everything
goes down the drain
and everything goes down the
drain
into the sewer
into the sewer
into the sewer

and the juicy
Georgia
peach
and the juicy
Georgia peach
and the juicy Georgia peach
is getting
a little
overripe
is getting a little
overripe
and a slight
feeling
of insecurity
is getting a little overripe,
and a slight feeling
of insecurity
and a slight feeling of insecurity,
that gradually
begins
to spiral
that gradually begins
to spiral
that gradually begins to spiral,
and the plug
in the bathtub
and the plug in the bathtub
gets pulled
gets pulled
and the plug in the bathtub gets
pulled,
and everything
goes down
the drain
and everything
goes down the drain
and everything goes down the
drain
into the sewer
into the sewer
into the sewer

The air
of unreality
The air of unreality
The air of unreality
was thick
was thick
was thick
here
was thick here
here
as President
Nixon
as President Nixon
as President Nixon,
on as beautiful
a day
on as beautiful a day
as anyone
could wish for
on as beautiful a day as anyone
could wish for
as anyone could wish for

He was too
drunk
He was too drunk
to crawl
out
He was too drunk to crawl out
to crawl out,
because
when
they finally
found him
because when they finally
found him
the next
day
because when they finally found
him
the next day

The air
of unreality
The air of unreality
The air of unreality
was thick
was thick
was thick
here
was thick here
here
as President
Nixon
as President Nixon
as President Nixon,
on as beautiful
a day
on as beautiful a day
as anyone
could wish for
on as beautiful a day as anyone
could wish for
as anyone could wish for

He was too
drunk
He was too drunk
to crawl
out
He was too drunk to crawl out
to crawl out,
because
when
they finally
found him
because when they finally
found him
the next
day
because when they finally found
him
the next day
the next day,

the next day,
he'd been
frozen
in the ice
he'd been frozen
in the ice
he'd been frozen in the ice
and was still
unconscious
and was still unconscious
and was still unconscious

Nearby
Nearby
Nearby
lay
the pelvis
of a man
lay
lay the pelvis of a man
severed
at the belt
the pelvis of a man
severed at the belt
severed at the belt,
two
white
thigh
bones
two white
thigh bones
two white thigh bones
sticking
sticking
sticking
from blood-soaked
trousers
sticking from blood-soaked trousers
from blood-soaked trousers

he'd been
frozen
in the ice
he'd been frozen
in the ice
he'd been frozen in the ice
and was still
unconscious
and was still unconscious
and was still unconscious

Nearby
Nearby
Nearby
lay
the pelvis
of a man
lay
lay the pelvis of a man
severed
at the belt
the pelvis of a man
severed at the belt
severed at the belt,
two
white
thigh
bones
two white
thigh bones
two white thigh bones
sticking
sticking
sticking
from blood-soaked
trousers
sticking from blood-soaked trousers
from blood-soaked trousers

A 30-year-old
A 30-year-old
unemployed
cook
unemployed cook
A 30-year-old unemployed cook
was charged
with murder
was charged with murder
yesterday
was charged with murder yes-
terday
for allegedly
beating
one
of his three
sons
for allegedly beating
one
of his three sons
for allegedly beating
one of his three sons
to death
to death
to death
in 1970
in 1970
in 1970
and then entombing
the boy's
body
and then entombing
the boy's body
and then entombing the boy's
body
with cement
and plaster
with cement and plaster
in a trunk
with cement and plaster in a
trunk
in a trunk
in a Bronx
basement
in a Bronx basement

A 30-year-old
unemployed
cook
unemployed cook
A 30-year-old unemployed cook
was charged
with murder
was charged with murder
yesterday
was charged with murder yes-
terday
for allegedly
beating
one
of his three
sons
for allegedly beating
one
of his three sons
for allegedly beating
one of his three sons
to death
to death
to death
in 1970
in 1970
in 1970
and then entombing
the boy's
body
and then entombing
the boy's body
and then entombing the boy's
body
with cement
and plaster
with cement and plaster
in a trunk
with cement and plaster in a
trunk
in a trunk
in a Bronx
basement
in a Bronx basement

A 30-year-old

everyone
is laughing
at you
everyone is laughing
at you
everyone is laughing at you,
and making
fun
of you
and making fun
of you
and making fun of you,
they're drunk
and stoned
and nasty
they're drunk and stoned
and nasty
they're drunk and stoned and
nasty,
and you're surrounded
and you're surrounded
by this terrifying
freak
show
and you're surrounded
by this terrifying
freak show
by this terrifying freak show,
and they're ridiculing
you
and they're ridiculing you
and they're ridiculing you,
and laughing
at you
and laughing at you
and laughing at you,
and you're
uptight
and you're uptight
and you're uptight
and you're uptight,
and you're really
tight
and you're really tight

is laughing
at you
everyone is laughing
at you
everyone is laughing at you,
and making
fun
of you
and making fun
of you
and making fun of you,
they're drunk
and stoned
and nasty
they're drunk and stoned
and nasty
they're drunk and stoned and
nasty,
and you're surrounded
and you're surrounded
by this terrifying
freak
show
and you're surrounded
by this terrifying
freak show
by this terrifying freak show,
and they're ridiculing
you
and they're ridiculing you
and they're ridiculing you,
and laughing
at you
and laughing at you
and laughing at you,
and you're
uptight
and you're uptight
and you're uptight
and you're uptight,
and you're really
tight
and you're really tight
and you're really tight,

everyone and you're really tight,

and you try
to smile
and you try to smile
and you try to smile,
but you can't
but you can't
but you can't,
and you can't
think
of anything
to say
to say
to anyone
and you can't think of anything
to say
to anyone
to anyone,
and nobody
will talk
to you
and nobody will talk
to you
and nobody will talk to you,
and you are confused
and lonely
and unhappy
and freaked out
and you are confused
and lonely and unhappy
and freaked out
and you are confused and lonely
and unhappy and freaked out,
and you just
want
to touch
somebody
and you just want
to touch somebody
and you just want to touch
somebody,
but you've forgotten
how
to do it
but you've forgotten
how to do it

to smile
and you try to smile
and you try to smile,
but you can't
but you can't
but you can't,
and you can't
think
of anything
to say
to say
to anyone
and you can't think of anything
to say
to anyone
to anyone,
and nobody
will talk
to you
and nobody will talk
to you
and nobody will talk to you,
and you are confused
and lonely
and unhappy
and freaked out
and you are confused
and lonely and unhappy
and freaked out
and you are confused and lonely
and unhappy and freaked out,
and you just
want
to touch
somebody
and you just want
to touch somebody
and you just want to touch
somebody,
but you've forgotten
how
to do it
but you've forgotten
how to do it
but you've forgotten how to do it,

and you try but you've forgotten how to do it,

and you just   want
want   and you just want
and you just want   and you just want
and you just want   to hold
to hold   somebody
somebody   to hold somebody
to hold somebody   to hold somebody,
to hold somebody,   and kiss
and kiss   somebody
somebody   and kiss somebody
and kiss somebody   and kiss somebody,
and kiss somebody,   and you want
and you want   to do it
to do it   and you want to do it
and you want to do it   and you want to do it,
and you want to do it,   and you are waiting
and you are waiting   and you are waiting
and you are waiting   in an airport
in an airport   in an airport,
in an airport,   in a Holiday
in a Holiday   Inn
Inn   in a Holiday Inn,
in a Holiday Inn,   in a Ford
in a Ford   Pinto
Pinto   in a Ford Pinto,
in a Ford Pinto,   in a Dodge
in a Dodge   truck
truck   in a Dodge truck,
in a Dodge truck,   in a television
in a television   set
set   in a television set
in a television set   in a television set,
in a television set,   and the Ajax
and the Ajax   woman
woman   and the Ajax woman
and the Ajax woman   is scrubbing
is scrubbing   away
away   is scrubbing away
is scrubbing away   at your heart
at your heart   and the Ajax woman is scrubbing
and the Ajax woman is scrubbing   away
away   at your heart
at your heart   at your heart,

and you just   at your heart,

until
there is nothing
left
until there is nothing
left
to work with
until there is nothing left
to work with,
and whatever
is left
and whatever is left
and whatever is left,
just goes
down
the drain
pipe
just goes down
the drain pipe
and it all
seems
to you
and it all
seems to you
and it all seems to you
like big
loss
like big loss
like big loss

A missing
man
A missing man
who apparently
was murdered
A missing man
who apparently was murdered
who apparently was murdered
is believed
buried

there is nothing
left
until there is nothing
left
to work with
until there is nothing left
to work with,
and whatever
is left
and whatever is left
and whatever is left,
just goes
down
the drain
pipe
just goes down
the drain pipe
and it all
seems
to you
and it all
seems to you
and it all seems to you
like big
loss
like big loss
like big loss

A missing
man
A missing man
who apparently
was murdered
A missing man
who apparently was murdered
who apparently was murdered
is believed
buried
is believed buried

until is believed buried

under
a mammoth
mountain
of garbage
under a mammoth
mountain of garbage
under a mammoth mountain of
garbage
and landfill
on Staten Island
and landfill on Staten Island,
where
his corpse
where his corpse
was dumped
months
ago
where his corpse was dumped
months ago
was dumped months ago
after
it was picked up
with the refuse
after it was picked up
with the refuse
after it was picked up with the refuse

the slight
dissatisfaction
the slight dissatisfaction
with the present
the slight dissatisfaction
with the present,
the lack
of satisfaction
the lack of satisfaction
the lack of satisfaction,
always
there
always there
always there,
always
getting
ready
always
getting ready
under

a mammoth
mountain
of garbage
under a mammoth
mountain of garbage
under a mammoth mountain of
garbage
and landfill
on Staten Island
and landfill on Staten Island,
where
his corpse
where his corpse
was dumped
months
ago
where his corpse was dumped
months ago
was dumped months ago
after
it was picked up
with the refuse
after it was picked up
with the refuse
after it was picked up with the refuse

the slight
dissatisfaction
the slight dissatisfaction
with the present
the slight dissatisfaction
with the present,
the lack
of satisfaction
the lack of satisfaction
the lack of satisfaction,
always
there
always there
always there,
always
getting
ready
always
getting ready
always getting ready,
always getting ready,

preparing
to do
it
preparing
to do it
preparing to do it,
but actually
you're only
always
getting
ready
but actually you're only
always getting ready
but actually you're only always
getting ready,
as if listening
to this poem
might be it
as if listening to this poem
might be it
as if listening to this poem might
be it,
but I wouldn't
bet
on it
but I wouldn't
bet on it
but I wouldn't bet on it,
I hope
you didn't
think
I hope you didn't think
you were going
to get
anything
out
of it
I hope you didn't think
you were going to get
anything out of it
you were going to get anything

to do
it
preparing
to do it
preparing to do it,
but actually
you're only
always
getting
ready
but actually you're only
always getting ready
but actually you're only always
getting ready,
as if listening
to this poem
might be it
as if listening to this poem
might be it
as if listening to this poem might
be it,
but I wouldn't
bet
on it
but I wouldn't
bet on it
but I wouldn't bet on it,
I hope
you didn't
think
I hope you didn't think
you were going
to get
anything
out
of it
I hope you didn't think
you were going to get
anything out of it
you were going to get anything
out of it,

preparing out of it,

you don't
even get
your money
back
you don't even get your money
back,
no refunds
no refunds
no refunds,
sorry
folks
sorry folks,
there are no
promises
there are no promises
there are no promises

it's a slow
wasting
disease
it's a slow
wasting disease
it's a slow wasting disease,
that lets
the mind
watch
that lets the mind watch
as the body
dies
that lets the mind watch
as the body dies
as the body dies

and that's
my conceptualization
and that's my conceptualization
and that's my conceptualization,
and if it isn't
so
and if it isn't so

you don't

even get
your money
back
you don't even get your money
back,
no refunds
no refunds
no refunds,
sorry
folks
sorry folks,
there are no
promises
there are no promises
there are no promises

it's a slow
wasting
disease
it's a slow
wasting disease
it's a slow wasting disease,
that lets
the mind
watch
that lets the mind watch
as the body
dies
that lets the mind watch
as the body dies
as the body dies

and that's
my conceptualization
and that's my conceptualization
and that's my conceptualization,
and if it isn't
so
and if it isn't so
and if it isn't so,

and if it isn't so,

then
it's one
big
mess
then it's one
big mess
then it's one big mess

an evangelist
an evangelist
an evangelist
was sewn
up
inside
a tom-tom
was sewn up
inside a tom-tom
was sewn up inside a tom-tom
and died
and died
and died
after
three
weeks
of torture
after three weeks
of torture
after three weeks of torture

Little
natural
pools
Little natural
pools
Little natural pools
were formed
by braces
of rocks
were formed
by braces of rocks

it's one
big
mess
then it's one
big mess
then it's one big mess

an evangelist
an evangelist
an evangelist
was sewn
up
inside
a tom-tom
was sewn up
inside a tom-tom
was sewn up inside a tom-tom
and died
and died
and died
after
three
weeks
of torture
after three weeks
of torture
after three weeks of torture

Little
natural
pools
Little natural
pools
Little natural pools
were formed
by braces
of rocks
were formed
by braces of rocks
were formed by braces of rocks,

then were formed by braces of rocks,

so we all
jumped
into the cold
water
so we all jumped
into the cold water
so we all jumped into the cold
water
and floated
on our backs
and floated on our backs
and floated on our backs
gazing
up
gazing up
gazing up
gazing up
at the soaring
volcanic
rock
walls
at the soaring
volcanic rock walls
at the soaring volcanic rock walls
of the canyon
of the canyon
of the canyon

You were
sick
You were sick
You were sick,
but you're not
sick
anymore
but you're not sick
but you're not sick anymore,
at least
you think so
at least you think so
at least you think so,
you think
you're alright
you think you're alright
you think you're alright

jumped
into the cold
water
so we all jumped
into the cold water
so we all jumped into the cold
water
and floated
on our backs
and floated on our backs
and floated on our backs
gazing
up
gazing up
gazing up
gazing up
at the soaring
volcanic
rock
walls
at the soaring
volcanic rock walls
at the soaring volcanic rock walls
of the canyon
of the canyon
of the canyon

You were
sick
You were sick
You were sick,
but you're not
sick
anymore
but you're not sick
but you're not sick anymore,
at least
you think so
at least you think so
at least you think so,
you think
you're alright
you think you're alright
you think you're alright

so we all

Vajra
Hell
Vajra Hell
Vajra Hell
is something
you did
wrong
is something
you did wrong
is something you did wrong,
is something
you really
did wrong
is something you really did
wrong,
and the result
and the result
has turned
into cancer
has turned into cancer
has turned into cancer,
and it's eating
your insides
out
and it's eating
your insides out
and it's eating your insides out,
your stomach
your stomach
and lungs
and lungs
and liver
and liver,
when
there's nothing
left
when there's
nothing left
but your skin
but your skin
when there's nothing left
but your skin,
it eats
your skin
it eats your skin

Hell
Vajra Hell
Vajra Hell
is something
you did
wrong
is something
you did wrong
is something you did wrong,
is something
you really
did wrong
is something you really did
wrong,
and the result
and the result
has turned
into cancer
has turned into cancer
has turned into cancer,
and it's eating
your insides
out
and it's eating
your insides out
and it's eating your insides out,
your stomach
your stomach
and lungs
and lungs
and liver
and liver,
when
there's nothing
left
when there's
nothing left
but your skin
but your skin
when there's nothing left
but your skin,
it eats
your skin
it eats your skin
it eats your skin,

Vajra it eats your skin,

then something
comes
from outside
then something
comes from outside
then something comes from
outside
and forms
and forms
a new
skin
and forms a new skin
a new skin,
and the cancer
and the cancer
and the cancer
continues
continues
to eat it
away
continues to eat it away
to eat it away,
and it has hurt
for so long
an it has hurt for so long
and it has hurt for so long,
it doesn't
hurt
anymore
it doesn't hurt
anymore
it doesn't hurt anymore,
and you haven't
cried
since
the beginning
and you haven't cried
since the beginning
and you haven't cried

comes
from outside
then something
comes from outside
then something comes from
outside
and forms
and forms
a new
skin
and forms a new skin
a new skin,
and the cancer
and the cancer
and the cancer
continues
continues
to eat it
away
continues to eat it away
to eat it away,
and it has hurt
for so long
an it has hurt for so long
and it has hurt for so long,
it doesn't
hurt
anymore
it doesn't hurt
anymore
it doesn't hurt anymore,
and you haven't
cried
since
the beginning
and you haven't cried
since the beginning
and you haven't cried
since the beginning,

then something since the beginning,

but you just
want
to cry
but you just want to cry
you just want
you just want
you just want
to cry
to cry
to cry
again
again
again,
but then
but then
you've forgotten
but then you've forgotten
you even
wanted to
you've forgotten you even
wanted to
you even wanted to,
you've forgotten
about cancer
you've forgotten about cancer
you've forgotten about cancer

the incredible
sweep
of the desert
the incredible sweep
of the desert
the incredible sweep of the desert,
of great
golden
mesas
of great golden mesas
with purple
shadows
with purple shadows
of great golden mesas

want
to cry
but you just want to cry
you just want
you just want
you just want
to cry
to cry
to cry
again
again
again,
but then
but then
you've forgotten
but then you've forgotten
you even
wanted to
you've forgotten you even
wanted to
you even wanted to,
you've forgotten
about cancer
you've forgotten about cancer
you've forgotten about cancer

the incredible
sweep
of the desert
the incredible sweep
of the desert
the incredible sweep of the desert,
of great
golden
mesas
of great golden mesas
with purple
shadows
with purple shadows
of great golden mesas
with purple shadows,

but you just with purple shadows,

and tremendous
stars
and tremendous stars
appearing
appearing
at dusk
and tremendous stars appearing
at dusk
from a turquoise
sky
at dusk from a turquoise sky
from a turquoise sky

the Buddhas
the Buddhas
the Buddhas
having transformed
themselves
into shellfish
having transformed themselves
into shellfish
having transformed themselves
into shellfish,
red
pearls
red pearls
red pearls
were produced
in their stomachs
were produced in their stomachs
were produced in their stomachs

He ground
the gods
He ground the gods
He ground the gods
together
with their guardians
together with their guardians
into dust
together with their guardians
into dust

stars
and tremendous stars
appearing
appearing
at dusk
and tremendous stars appearing
at dusk
from a turquoise
sky
at dusk from a turquoise sky
from a turquoise sky

the Buddhas
the Buddhas
the Buddhas
having transformed
themselves
into shellfish
having transformed themselves
into shellfish
having transformed themselves
into shellfish,
red
pearls
red pearls
red pearls
were produced
in their stomachs
were produced in their stomachs
were produced in their stomachs

He ground
the gods
He ground the gods
He ground the gods
together
with their guardians
together with their guardians
into dust
together with their guardians
into dust
into dust,

and tremendous into dust,

when
the king
when the king
tried
to burn
Him
alive
when the king tried to burn Him
alive
tried to burn Him alive,
by his magical
powers
by his magical powers
by his magical powers
He transformed
He transformed
the middle
of the fire
into a lake
He transformed the middle of
the fire
into a lake
the middle of the fire into a lake,
He is born
of a lotus
He is born of a lotus
He is born of a lotus,
the Guru
the Guru
who roars
like a lion
the Guru who roars like a lion
who roars like a lion,
who is like
the rays
of the sun
who is like the rays
of the sun
who is like the rays of the sun,
the Guru
the Guru
the Guru
who is the Lotus-born
Vajra
who is the Lotus-born Vajra
who is the Lotus-born Vajra

when
the king
when the king
tried
to burn
Him
alive
when the king tried to burn Him
alive
tried to burn Him alive,
by his magical
powers
by his magical powers
by his magical powers
He transformed
He transformed
the middle
of the fire
into a lake
He transformed the middle of
the fire
into a lake
the middle of the fire into a lake,
He is born
of a lotus
He is born of a lotus
He is born of a lotus,
the Guru
the Guru
who roars
like a lion
the Guru who roars like a lion
who roars like a lion,
who is like
the rays
of the sun
who is like the rays
of the sun
who is like the rays of the sun,
the Guru
the Guru
the Guru
who is the Lotus-born
Vajra
who is the Lotus-born Vajra
who is the Lotus-born Vajra

(1974)

it's nighttime
it's nighttime,
it's just
one
more
night
again
it's just one
more night
it's just one more night again
again
again,
and you're home
and you're home,
lying
on the couch
lying on the couch
with the blue
flowers
with the blue flowers,
there's
nothing
to do
there's nothing
there's nothing
there's nothing
to do
there's nothing to do,
and you can't
be with
anybody
for another
12 hours
and you can't
take it
one
more
minute
and you can't take it
and you can't take it one more

it's nighttime
it's nighttime,
it's just
one
more
night
again
it's just one
more night
it's just one more night again
again
again,
and you're home
and you're home,
lying
on the couch
lying on the couch
with the blue
flowers
with the blue flowers,
there's
nothing
to do
there's nothing
there's nothing
there's nothing
to do
there's nothing to do,
and you can't
be with
anybody
for another
12 hours
and you can't
take it
one
more
minute
and you can't take it
and you can't take it one more
minute

minute
one more minute,
and you hate
being
alone
and you hate
being alone
and you hate being alone,
you're shaking
you're shaking
shaking,
it's out
of control
it's out of control
it's out of control,
contagious
poison
contagious poison
contagious poison

it's a TV
quiz
show
it's a TV quiz show,
Strike
It Rich
Strike It Rich
Strike It Rich,
The Price
Is Right
The Price Is Right
The Price Is Right,
The $25,000
Pyramid
The $25,000 Pyramid,
Concentration
Concentration
Concentration,
you're always
watching
you're always

one more minute,
and you hate
being
alone
and you hate
being alone
and you hate being alone,
you're shaking
you're shaking
shaking,
it's out
of control
it's out of control
it's out of control,
contagious
poison
contagious poison
contagious poison

it's a TV
quiz
show
it's a TV quiz show,
Strike
It Rich
Strike It Rich
Strike It Rich,
The Price
Is Right
The Price Is Right
The Price Is Right,
The $25,000
Pyramid
The $25,000 Pyramid,
Concentration
Concentration,
Concentration,
you're always
watching
you're always
sitting

sitting
there watching
you're always only
sitting there watching,
and you get
the big
chance
and you get the big chance,
you get
you get
up
up
up
there
you get up there,
and you win
a vacuum
cleaner
and you win a vacuum cleaner,
a sewing
machine
a sewing machine,
and a complete
set
of Teflon
cooking
pots,
and you blow
it
and you blow it
and you blow it
and you blow it,
you guessed
wrong
you guessed wrong
you guessed wrong
and they take
all
the prizes
away
and they take all the prizes away,

there watching
you're always only
sitting there watching,
and you get
the big
chance
and you get the big chance,
you get
you get
up
up
up
there
you get up there,
and you win
a vacuum
cleaner
and you win a vacuum cleaner,
a sewing
machine
a sewing machine,
and a complete
set
of Teflon
cooking
pots,
and you blow
it
and you blow it
and you blow it
and you blow it,
you guessed
wrong
you guessed wrong
you guessed wrong
and they take
all
the prizes
away
and they take all the prizes away,
and the consolation

and the consolation
prize
and the consolation prize
is dinner
for two
in a Chinese
restaurant
is dinner for two in a Chinese restaurant,
and you almost
won
and you almost
and you almost won
won
a new
car
a new car
a new car,
Buick
dedicated
to the freedom
in everyone,
a yacht
a yacht,
a trip
around
the world
a trip around the world
you almost
won
the million
dollar
lottery
the million dollar
lottery
the million dollar lottery,
you really
wanted
you really wanted
everything
so much
you really wanted everything so much

prize
and the consolation prize
is dinner
for two
in a Chinese
restaurant
is dinner for two in a Chinese restaurant
and you almost
won
and you almost
and you almost won
won
a new
car
a new car
a new car,
Buick
dedicated
to the freedom
in everyone,
a yacht
a yacht,
a trip
around
the world
a trip around the world,
you almost
won
the million
dollar
lottery
the million dollar
lottery
the million dollar lottery,
you really
wanted
you really wanted
everything
so much
you really wanted everything so much
everything so much,

everything so much,
and if that isn't
bad
enough
and if that isn't
bad enough
and if that isn't bad enough,
everything
is taken
away
again
everything
everything is taken away
is taken away
again,
the inconceivable
wipe-out
the inconceivable wipe-out
the inconceivable wipe-out,
and you're dead
and you're dead
and you're dead
and you're dead,
they pull
the sheet
over
your head
they pull the sheet
they pull the sheet over your head,
and take you
to Cook's
Funeral
Home
and they take you
and they take you
to Cook's funeral home,
where
they stick
needles
into you
where they stick needles into you

and if that isn't
bad
enough
and if that isn't
bad enough
and if that isn't bad enough,
everything
is taken
away
again
everything
everything is taken away
is taken away,
again,
the inconceivable
wipe-out
the inconceivable wipe-out
the inconceivable wipe-out,
and you're dead
and you're dead
and you're dead
and you're dead,
they pull
the sheet
over
your head
they pull the sheet
they pull the sheet over your head,
and take you
to Cook's
Funeral
Home
and they take you
and they take you
to Cook's funeral home,
where
they stick
needles
into you
where they stick needles into you
and this machine

and this machine
sucks
all
your blood
out
and this machine sucks
all your blood out,
and pumps
and pumps
formaldehyde
into your body
formaldehyde into your body,
and fills
your very own body
with embalming
fluid

from
the center
from the center
of your heart
from the center of your heart
of your heart
rises
rises
rises
rises
the purity
the purity
the purity
and clarity
rises the purity and clarity
and clarity,
in the center
of your heart
where
it's always
been,
and it's hard
not
to freak out

sucks
all
your blood
out
and this machine sucks
all your blood out,
and pumps
and pumps
formaldehyde
into your body
formaldehyde into your body,
and fills
your very own body
with embalming
fluid

from
the center
from the center
of your heart
from the center of your heart
of your heart
rises
rises
rises
rises
the purity
the purity
the purity
and clarity
rises the purity and clarity
and clarity,
in the center
of your heart
where
it's always
been,
and it's hard
not

and it's hard not to freak out,
you've always
freaked out
when
it gets
down
to the nitty-gritty,
you're getting
out
of your body
you're getting out
of your body
you're getting out of your body,
and light
and light
and light
vomits
vomits
out
of your mouth
and light vomits out of your mouth
out of your mouth,

peeling
off
a rubber
suit
peeling off
a rubber suit
peeling off a rubber suit,
and there's
this coffin
and there's this coffin,
all
these people
talking
all these people talking
talking,
and praying
and praying
and praying,

to freak out
and it's hard not to freak out,
you've always
you've always freaked out,
when
it gets
down
to the nitty-gritty,
you're getting
out
of your body
you're getting out
of your body
you're getting out of your body,
and light
and light
and light
vomits
vomits
out
of your mouth
and light vomits out of your mouth
out of your mouth,
peeling
off
a rubber
suit
peeling off
a rubber suit
peeling off a rubber suit,
and there's
this coffin
and there's this coffin,
all
these people
talking
all these people talking
talking,
and praying
and praying
and praying,

from **SHIT PISS BLOOD PUS AND BRAINS, 1977**

and chattering
and chattering
and chattering,
it could
almost
be a nightmare
it could almost be a nightmare,
if it weren't
such a joke
if it weren't such a joke
if it weren't such a joke,
and it's a lighter
shade
than pale
it's a lighter
shade than pale
it's a lighter shade than pale,
and there's
no regrets
and there's no regrets
and there's no regrets,
and you are nothing
and you are nothing
and you are nothing,
unwavering
unwavering
unwavering,
and in a snap
of the fingers

clear
clear
clear,
vacuous
vacuous
vacuous,
without
duality
without duality,
transparent

and chattering
and chattering
and chattering,
it could
almost
be a nightmare
it could almost be a nightmare,
if it weren't
such a joke
if it weren't such a joke
if it weren't such a joke,
and it's a lighter
shade
than pale
it's a lighter
shade than pale
it's a lighter shade than pale,
and there's
no regrets
and there's no regrets
and there's no regrets,

and you are nothing
and you are nothing
and you are nothing,
unwavering
unwavering
unwavering,
and in a snap
of the fingers

clear
clear
clear,
vacuous
vacuous
vacuous,
without
duality
without duality,
transparent

transparent
transparent,
timeless
timeless
timeless,
uncompounded
uncompounded
uncompounded,
unimpeded
unimpeded
unimpeded,
colorless
colorless
colorless,
naked
naked
naked
naked,
immaculate
immaculate
immaculate,
not
made
of anything
not made
of anything
not made of anything,
being
being
being
void
void
void
being
void
being void
being void
unchanging
from the beginning
unchanging from the beginning
unchanging from the beginning,

transparent
transparent,
timeless
timeless
timeless,
uncompounded
uncompounded
uncompounded,
unimpeded
unimpeded
unimpeded,
colorless
colorless
colorless,
naked
naked
naked
naked,
immaculate
immaculate
immaculate,
not
made
of anything
not made
of anything
not made of anything,
being
being
being
void
void
void
being
void
being void
being void
unchanging
from the beginning
unchanging from the beginning
unchanging from the beginning,

***from* SHIT PISS BLOOD PUS AND BRAINS, 1977**

without
without
beginning,
middle
or end
beginning, middle or end,
without
birth
or death
without birth or death,
without
passing
away
or changing
without passing away or changing,
without
anything
that can be
indicated
without anything that can be indicated,
without
words
without words
without words,
not
to be realized
through
effort
not to be realized
through effort
not to be realized through effort,
without
anything
to be done
without anything
to be done
without anything to be done,
inconceivable
inconceivable
inconceivable

without
without
beginning,
middle
or end
beginning, middle or end,
without
birth
or death
without birth or death,
without
passing
away
or changing
without passing away or changing,
without
anything
that can be
indicated
without anything that can be indicated,
without
words
without words
without words,
not
to be realized
through
effort
not to be realized
through effort
not to be realized through effort,
without
anything
to be done
without anything
to be done
without anything to be done,
inconceivable
inconceivable
inconceivable

and unceasing
in flow

We
all
We all
went
to sleep
last
night
went to sleep
We all went to sleep last night
last night,
and had dream
and had dreams
went to sleep last night,
and had dreams,
good
and bad
dreams
good and bad dreams,
happy
happy
happy
and suffering
and suffering
and suffering
dreams
dreams
dreams,
and now
and now
and now,
we are
all
here
we are all here
now
we are all here now
now,

and unceasing
in flow

We
all
We all
went
to sleep
last
night
went to sleep
We all went to sleep last night
last night,
and had dreams
and had dreams
went to sleep last night,
and had dreams,
good
and bad
dreams
good and bad dreams,
happy
happy
happy
and suffering
and suffering
and suffering
dreams
dreams
dreams,
and now
and now
and now,
we are
all
here
we are all here
now
we are all here now
now,

***from* SHIT PISS BLOOD PUS AND BRAINS, 1977**

where
are the places
you visited
in your dreams
where are the places
you visited in your dreams,
where
did
your dreams
go
where did
your dreams go
where did your dreams go?

where
are the places
you visited
in your dreams
where are the places
you visited in your dreams,
where
did
your dreams
go
where did
your dreams go
where did your dreams go?

(1975)

EATING THE SKY

I don't
know
what
you've been
doing
today
I don't know what
you've been doing today,
but today
was one
of the worst
days
of my life
but today was one
of the worst days of my life
but today was one of the worst
days of my life,
you're walking
down
2nd Avenue
coming to
St. Marks Place
you're walking down 2nd Avenue
coming to St. Marks Place,
and all these
street
junkies
and whores
all these street junkies and whores,
and all
these straight
people

going
to work
and all these straight people
going to work,
ants
coming out
of the ground
at Astor
Place
ants coming out of the ground
at Astor Place,
and why
is everybody
so ugly
and why is everybody
so ugly
and why is everybody so ugly

I know
we haven't
been together
for a long
time
I know we haven't been together
for a long time,
and you're being
warm,
hospitable,
and gracious
and you're being, warm, hospitable,
and gracious,
you're cooking
dinner
you're cooking dinner,
and thank you

for the cracker
and cheese
and thank you for the cracker and cheese,
we're sitting
here
drinking
Scotch
and smoking
a joint
we're sitting here drinking Scotch
and smoking a joint,
the thought
of being
here
for 6 more
hours
the thought of being here
for 6 more hours,
I don't
ever
want
to be here
again
I don't ever
want to be
here again
I don't ever want
to be here again
I don't ever want to be here again,
I just want
to get
away
from you
I just want to get way from you,
it's Pasadena,

baby,
and how
can I
get out
the back

it's sad
to say
cause you are
my friends
it's sad to say cause you are my friends,
but I hate
every
moment
being here
with you
but I hate every moment being here
with you,
it's a complete
waste
of time,
cause
I've been
through
this one
before
cause I've been through
this one before
cause I've been through this one before

you do
nothing
but rip
off
whatever

is being
given
you do nothing but rip off
whatever is being given,
and you wake
up
and you wake up
you remember
you are dreaming
you remember you are dreaming
you wake up and you remember you are dreaming,
you were dreaming
you were dreaming
you were dreaming
you were only dreaming,
wake up
you're dreaming
wake up you're dreaming
wake up you're dreaming,
oh no,
do I
look
like that
oh no, do I
look like that
oh no, do I look like that

I'm walking
straight
ahead
I'm walking straight ahead
and I'm wearing
black
boots
and I'm wearing black boots,

black
and mean,
heart
breakers,
taking
my love
and leaving me
behind
taking my love
and leaving me behind
taking my love and leaving me behind

you're walking
proud
you're walking proud
you're walking proud,
you're walking
on a marble
floor
your walking on a marble floor,
in the Hotel
Pierre,
you're on
a high
roll
you're on a high roll,
your body
is on a high roll,
and I'm glued
to the saddle
and I'm glued to the saddle,
I'm playing
hard
ball
I'm playing

hard ball
I'm playing hard ball,
I want
it all
now
I want it
all now
I want it all now,
and nothing
less
and nothing less
and nothing less,
we're American
Airlines,
doing what
we do
best,
I don't
know
where
I am
when
I'm standing
here
I don't know where
I am when
I'm standing here
I don't know where I am
when I'm standing here,
and I get
great
pleasure
not knowing
where
I am

and I get great pleasure
not knowing where I am,
in between
your breaths
in between your breaths
where
there is
no subject
or object,
no concepts

I just
want you
to hold
my hand
I just want you
to hold my hand
I just want you to hold my hand,
cause
I'm in
Calcutta,
India,
cause I'm in Calcutta, India,
palm
trees
and air
pollution
palm trees and air pollution,
and everywhere
you turn
someone's
trying
to hustle
money
from you

and everywhere you turn
someone's trying to hustle money from you,
air pollution
worse
than New York
could dream
possible,
sucking in
the carbon
monoxide
sucking in the carbon monoxide,
like I'm sucking
a joint,
I'm staying
in a hotel
with wall-to-wall
gold
carpets
I'm staying in a hotel
with wall-to-wall gold carpets,
scotch
whiskey
and Nepali
hash
scotch whiskey and Nepali hash,
room
service
is going to
bring me
a hamburger
room service is going
to bring me a hamburger
and a chocolate
fudge
ice cream

sundae
and a chocolate fudge ice cream sundae,
the closed
circuit
push-button
Muzak
radio
the closed circuit push-button
Muzak radio
is playing
nobody
sings
a love
song
quite like
you do
nobody sings
a love song
quite like you do
nobody sings a love song quite like you do,
you are in Calcutta,
and the beggars
are grabbing
at you
and the beggars are grabbing at you,
it's poverty,
Mr. President,
and the lepers
alongside you
on the pavements
are like
my honey
and the lepers alongside you
on the pavement
are like my honey,

cruising
Christopher
Street
cruising
Christopher Street
cruising Christopher Street,
you are the worst
lover
I've ever had
you are the worst lover I've ever had,
I never
put my head
on your shoulder
I never put my head on your shoulder,
he's a dirty
schizoid
he's a dirty schizoid,
cool-aid
punch,
poison,
ugliness
and disappointment
cool-aid punch, poison,
ugliness and disappointment
cool-aid punch, poison, ugliness
and disappointment

I lost
my job
2 years
ago
I lost my job 2 years ago,
I drive
a truck
I drive a truck,

they took
my house
and my car
away
they took my house and my car away,
we're living
in this apartment
we're living in this apartment,
I never
thought
it would come
to this
I never thought it would come to this,
and I'm scared
of dying
and I'm scared of dying
and I'm scared of dying
I keep
thinking
about
the same
thing
over
and over
again
I keep thinking about the same thing
over and over again,
I keep
repeating
in my head
what I
said to you
I keep repeating in my head
what I said to you,
the same

sentence,
I go
first
cabin
I go first cabin,
you're staying
in the Grand
Hotel
you're staying in the Grand Hotel,
hamburgers
and fries
and cherry pies
hamburgers and fries and cherry pies,
and you're getting
fat
when you put
your pants
on
and you're getting fat
when you put your pants on,
cause
you gotta
make it
pay
cause you gotta make it pay,
like my Daddy
once said,
"It's trying
to put
50 pounds
of mud
in a 5 pound
bag
it's trying to put 50 pounds of mud
in a 5 pound bag"

in the morning
when I'm
shaving
in the morning when I'm shaving,
and I cut
myself
and I cut myself
and I cut myself,
I know it's
going to be
a bad
day
I know it's going
to be a bad day
I know it's going to be a bad day,
when I
go out
of this house
when I go out of this house,
we gotta have
security
we gotta have security,
now you
call for
a limo
now you call for a limo,
Dav-el
Livery
and say
I want
a stretch
Dav-el Livery and say I want a stretch,
I'm having
myself

a couple
of lovers
I'm having myself a couple of lovers,
but I want
to call
a meeting
of all
my advisors
I want to call a meeting
of all my advisors,
cause I
want to say,
I'm in
trouble
I'm in trouble
I'm in trouble
I'm in trouble
I'm in trouble,
so take
this job
and shove it
I ain't
working
here
no more
so take this job and shove it
I ain't working here no more,
booze,
cocaine,
dope,
and cigarettes
booze, cocaine,
dope, and cigarettes,
booze, cocaine, dope, and cigarettes
ruthless

and always
right
ruthless and always right
you are staying
in a motel
in Milwaukee
you are staying in a motel in Milwaukee
and you're smoking
a cigarette
and you're smoking a cigarette,
and I'm gonna
get myself
another drink
and I'm gonna get myself another drink,
and the radio
is playing,
you just
have to wait,
love don't
come easy
you just have to wait,
love don't come easy
you just have to wait, love
don't come easy,
it's more
than you might
have expected,
so put out
the do not
disturb
sign
so put out the do not disturb sign
and lock
your door,
it's a mistake

being here
it's a mistake being here
it's a mistake being here,
and when
you wake up,
it's breakfast
in a foreign
country
it's breakfast in a foreign country,
you are in
Paris,
France
you are in Paris, France,
and everything
on the street
is straight
and everything on the street
is straight
and everything on the street is straight,
like when
you're sitting
in a telephone
booth
just after
we've hung
up
like when you're sitting
in a telephone booth
just after we've hung up,
completely
boring
completely boring
and completely
sad
and completely sad,

and slightly
threatening
and slightly threatening
and slightly threatening and completely sad,
you're waiting
on the platform
in Manhasset
you're waiting on the platform
in Manhasset
for the Long Island
Railroad
to come
take you
back
to New York
for the Long Island Railroad
to come take you back to New York,
you're smoking
a joint
you're smoking a joint,
cause you
just had
dinner
with your mother
and dad
cause you just had dinner
with your mother and dad,
and I know
I'm not
going to be
doing
this
for the rest
of my life
and I know I'm not going to be doing this

for the rest of my life,
but when
is it
going
to end,
I'm always
excruciatingly
waiting here,
I'm always excruciatingly waiting here,
what
I want
what I want
what I want
what I want
you got
you got
you got
what I
want,
only
you
only you,
and it's not
here
on the Manhasset
platform,
but when
I'm with you
it feels
the same
as this
but when I'm with you
it feels the same as this,
and you
and I

have been told,
that this
suffering
that this suffering
is display
is display
is display,
pure
phenomena,
and there is no
impure
phenomena,
neither
pure
nor impure,
and completely pure

so I ain't
gonna get
any more
than the Manhasset
platform,
surrendering to the Manhasset platform,
is what
turns into
bliss
is what turns
into bliss
is what turns into bliss
riding
a quarter
horse
in a rhinestone
rodeo
riding a quarter horse in a rhinestone rodeo,

you're on
in 3
minutes
you're on in 3 minutes,
oh say
can you
see
by the dawn's
early
light
oh say can you see by the dawn's early light
that our flag
was still
there
that our flag was still there,
you're waiting
in your dentist's
office
you're waiting in your dentist's office,
you were
on time
you were on time
you were on time,
but he's
in there
with another
patient
but he's in there with another patient,
you pick up
Time
Magazine
you pick up Time Magazine
and there's
Jasper
Johns

on the cover
and there's Jasper Johns on the cover,
you're sitting
there
in the dentist
chair
you're sitting there in the dentist chair,
and this old
man
who looks like
Pope John
Paul II
and this old man who looks like
Pope John Paul II,
and his hands
are shaking
and his hands are shaking,
and he's talking
about his daughter
who's married
to someone
in New Jersey
who owns
a Cessna
airplane
and he's talking about his daughter
who's married to someone in New Jersey
who owns a Cessna airplane,
and his hands
are shaking
and his hands are shaking
and you think
the drill
got your
cheek

and you think the drill
got your cheek
and you think the drill got your cheek

relaxing
in emptiness,
you only
can become
enlightened
by your own
phenomena
you only can become enlightened
by your own phenomena,
eating
the sky
eating the sky
eating the sky
eating the sky
eating the sky

but the world
ran out
of love
tonight
but the world ran out
of love tonight
but the world ran out of love tonight,
hopelessly
devoted
to you
hopelessly devoted to you

but where
did it
come from
but where did it

come from
but where did it come from,
what
am I
supposed to be
looking for
what am I
supposed to be looking for
what am I supposed to be looking for,
it's a clear
picture
it's a clear picture
it's a clear picture,
transparent
and luminous
endlessly
arising
phenomena
endlessly arising phenomena

we've reached
our cruising
altitude
of 37,000
feet,
the cabin
is pressurized
for your comfort
the cabin is pressurized
for your comfort,
our flight
will take us
over Denver,
Omaha,
Chicago,

and north of Cleveland,
you're walking
down
the aisle
to your seat
you're walking down
the aisle to your seat,
with all
these people
on either
side of you
with all these people
on either side of you,
and the airline
hostess
and the airline hostess
is looking
in your eyes
and smiling
is looking in your eyes
and smiling
is looking in your eyes and smiling,
can I
offer you
a drink,
Coca Cola,
7 Up
Coca Cola, 7 Up,
or an alcoholic
beverage
is a $1.50,
I'm sleeping
single
in a double
bed

I'm sleeping single
in a double bed
I'm sleeping single in a double bed,
thinking
over things
what
I should
have said
thinking over things what I should have said,
I'm stretching
my legs
I'm stretching my legs,
Mamas,
don't let
your babies
grow up
to be cowboys,

and you are
completely
worn out
and you are completely
worn out
and you are completely worn out,
tired,
I said,
and you're riding
in Alice's
car
and you're riding in Alice's car,
you're sitting
next
to Charlie
you're sitting next to Charlie,
and anything

anyone
is saying
is dragging
their nails
across
the black board
and anything anyone is saying
is dragging their nails
across the blackboard,
you're sitting
in the car
next to
Bob
you're sitting in the car
next to Bob,
and I don't
want
anybody's
shoulder
or leg
to touch me
and I don't want anybody's
shoulder or leg to touch me
and I don't want anybody's shoulder or leg
to touch me,

the clarity
inside
this car
the clarity inside this car,
I mean
the visuals,
is so clear
is so clear
is so clear,

the clarity
of my hate
the clarity of my hate,
and if I wasn't
grasping
the hate
and if I wasn't grasping the hate,
without
making
concepts
about it
without making concepts about it,
not holding
on
not holding on
not holding on,
is transforming
anger
into the clarity
of wisdom
mind,
going
up
in smoke
going up
in smoke
going up in smoke
going up in smoke
going up in smoke
and we got
no hope.

(1978)

from PUT YOUR EAR TO STONE OPEN YOUR HEART TO SKY

...

give me
another
sniff
cause
I'm cruising
give me another sniff cause I'm cruising
I'm going
upstairs
to see
what's
happening
there
I'm going upstairs
to see what's
happening there
I'm going upstairs to see
what's happening there,
I'm going to
make you
love me
I'm going to make
you love me
I'm going to make you love me,
the duration
of the relationship
of black
flies
making love
in June,

a pig
party,
I love
broad
staircases,
hurry up
and make
your move
hurry up
and make your move
hurry up and make your move,
I can't
wait
no longer
I can't wait no longer,
no romance
just want
to dance
I want to
go check
out
downstairs
I want to go check out downstairs,
but you keep
keep not
looking at me
but you keep not looking at me,
and somebody
else said
No
and somebody else
said No
and somebody else said No,
let's go
around
behind

the bar
let's go around behind the bar,
you're making
it with
somebody else
you're making it with somebody else,
and I'm not
looking at you
cause I
don't want
to seem
uncool
and get
beat up
and I'm not looking at you
cause I don't want to seem uncool
and get beat up,
like when
you're walking
down
the sidewalk
looking at
a building
you used to
live in
like when you're walking down the sidewalk
looking at a building you used to live in,
I always
lost
everything
I got,
so there ain't
no reason
to suppose
I'm not

losing
everything
now
I always lost everything I got,
so there ain't no reason to supposed
I'm not losing everything now,
I'm gonna
walk
that way
cause it's
clockwise
and good
luck
like inside
my heart,
if I said you
had a beautiful
body
would you
hold it
against me
if I said you had a beautiful body
would you hold it against me
If I said you had a beautiful body would
you hold it against me,
you're riding
First
Class
On United
Airlines
you're riding First Class
on United Airlines,
and the beautiful
smiling
lady

in the designer
uniform
keeps
filling up
your Bloody
Mary
with doubles,
and I got
the earphones
on
and I got the earphones on,
I really
got that feeling
that I'll
love you
for a long
long
time
I really got the feeling
that I'll love you
for a long long time
I really got the feeling that
I'll love you for a long long time,
and I keep
thinking about
writing
down
a list
of things
I gotta do
tomorrow
in New York
and I keep thinking about writing down
a list of things I gotta do
tomorrow in New York,

a sip
of vodka
I'm putting
Crisco
on my hand,
give me some popper
a sip of vodka,
I'm putting Crisco on my hand,
give me some popper,
you're making
the right
move
you're making the right move,
being in
the right
place
at the right
time,
being in the right place
at the right time,
all
I want
is to lay
here
next
to you
all I want is to lay
here holding you,
empty
blondes,
and/or dark,
hungry
and tough
empty blondes,
and/or dark, hungry and tough,

and ugly
I don't want
to count
the number
of people
I've made
it with
in this place
I don't want to count the number
of people I've made it with
in this place,
you never
realize
how
good
something is
until you
haven't
got it,
you realize
while you're
holding him,
how good something is
until you haven't got it,
treacherous,
dreamy,
full
of deceit,
and lustful
treacherous, dreamy, full of deceit,
and lustful,
I'm taking
a little
pleasure
in a little bit

of love,
I could
watch you
forever
putting
your make-up
on
I could watch you forever
putting your make-up on,
just
sitting
here
listening
to your honey
talk
you sitting here
listening to your honey talk,
or you complaining
or you complaining
or you complaining,
I just
know
if I belonged
in heaven,
your words
would sound
like a song,
and I'm going
downstairs
and I'm going downstairs,
cause I'm
going to be
lucky
tonight
cause I'm going

to be lucky tonight
cause I'm going to be lucky tonight,
I want to
see what's
happening
on the 3rd floor,
I haven't
been up
there
for one hour
I want to see what's happening
on the 3rd floor,
you gotta go
fast
you gotta go fast,
cause it's
always
slow
up
here,
I'm going
to get it
I'm going to get it
I'm going to
get it,
cruising
dead
boys
cruising
dead
boys
cruising dead boys,
who won't
believe
they're dead,

and keep
walking
around
remembering
they're walking
around
and keep walking around,
remembering they're walking around,
believing
your body
there
so much
it's there,
and I see
ya
and I feel ya
and I see ya and I feel ya,
cruising
dead boys,
hungry
ghosts
I'm hungry
hungry ghosts I'm hungry,
and everybody
loves
a Percodan
cause
they know
a Percodan
kills
pain,
and you're nothing
but a hungry
stray
dog

stalking
trash
cans
on Amsterdam Avenue
you're nothing but a hungry stray dog
stalking trash cans on Amsterdam Avenue,
when
I die
I may not
go to heaven,
cause I
don't know
if they let
cowboys in
when I die I may not go to heaven,
cause I don't know
if they let cowboys in,
if they don't
just let me
go to Texas
if they don't
just let me go to Texas
if they don't just let me go to Texas,
Texas
is as close
as I've been
...

(1979)

GRASPING AT EMPTINESS

<table>
<tr><td align="right">You are walking</td><td>You are walking</td></tr>
<tr><td align="right">down</td><td>down</td></tr>
<tr><td align="right">Lafayette</td><td>Lafayette</td></tr>
<tr><td align="right">Street</td><td>Street</td></tr>
<tr><td></td><td>you are walking down</td></tr>
<tr><td></td><td>Lafayette Street</td></tr>
<tr><td align="right">and your face</td><td>and your face</td></tr>
<tr><td align="right">twists</td><td>twists</td></tr>
<tr><td align="right">up</td><td>up</td></tr>
<tr><td></td><td>and your face twists up</td></tr>
<tr><td align="right">and starts</td><td>and starts</td></tr>
<tr><td align="right">crying</td><td>crying</td></tr>
<tr><td></td><td>and starts crying</td></tr>
<tr><td></td><td>and starts crying,</td></tr>
<tr><td></td><td>you are walking down Lafayette Street</td></tr>
<tr><td></td><td>and your face twists up and starts crying,</td></tr>
<tr><td align="right">turn</td><td>turn</td></tr>
<tr><td align="right">your face</td><td>your face</td></tr>
<tr><td align="right">to the wall</td><td>to the wall</td></tr>
<tr><td></td><td>turn your face to the wall</td></tr>
<tr><td align="right">so nobody'll</td><td>so nobody'll</td></tr>
<tr><td align="right">see</td><td>see</td></tr>
<tr><td></td><td>so nobody'll see,</td></tr>
<tr><td align="right">there's</td><td>there's</td></tr>
<tr><td align="right">tears</td><td>tears</td></tr>
<tr><td align="right">running</td><td>running</td></tr>
<tr><td align="right">down</td><td>down</td></tr>
<tr><td align="right">your cheeks</td><td>your cheeks</td></tr>
<tr><td></td><td>there's tears running down your cheeks,</td></tr>
<tr><td align="right">don't</td><td>don't</td></tr>
<tr><td align="right">hold on</td><td>hold on</td></tr>
<tr><td></td><td>don't hold on,</td></tr>
</table>

<table>
<tr><td align="right">cause</td><td>cause</td></tr>
<tr><td align="right">I'm already</td><td>I'm already</td></tr>
<tr><td align="right">gone</td><td>gone</td></tr>
<tr><td></td><td>cause I'm already gone;</td></tr>
<tr><td align="right">and there ain't</td><td>and there ain't</td></tr>
<tr><td align="right">nothing</td><td>nothing</td></tr>
<tr><td align="right">worse</td><td>worse</td></tr>
<tr><td align="right">in a relationship</td><td>in a relationship</td></tr>
<tr><td></td><td>and there ain't nothing worse</td></tr>
<tr><td></td><td>in a relationship</td></tr>
<tr><td align="right">than stupidity</td><td>than stupidity</td></tr>
<tr><td></td><td>than stupidity</td></tr>
<tr><td></td><td>than stupidity</td></tr>
<tr><td></td><td>than stupidity,</td></tr>
<tr><td align="right">you're so</td><td>you're so</td></tr>
<tr><td align="right">fucking</td><td>fucking</td></tr>
<tr><td align="right">up tight</td><td>up tight</td></tr>
<tr><td></td><td>you're so fucking</td></tr>
<tr><td></td><td>up tight</td></tr>
<tr><td></td><td>you're so fucking up tight,</td></tr>
<tr><td align="right">blind</td><td>blind</td></tr>
<tr><td align="right">ignorance</td><td>ignorance</td></tr>
<tr><td></td><td>blind ignorance</td></tr>
<tr><td></td><td>blind ignorance,</td></tr>
<tr><td align="right">and no matter</td><td>and no matter</td></tr>
<tr><td align="right">how</td><td>how</td></tr>
<tr><td align="right">much</td><td>much</td></tr>
<tr><td align="right">I love</td><td>I love</td></tr>
<tr><td align="right">fucking you</td><td>fucking you</td></tr>
<tr><td></td><td>no matter how I love fucking you</td></tr>
<tr><td align="right">no matter how much I love</td><td>no matter how much I love</td></tr>
<tr><td align="right">making love to you,</td><td>making love to you,</td></tr>
<tr><td align="right">I can't</td><td>I can't</td></tr>
<tr><td align="right">stand</td><td>stand</td></tr>
<tr><td align="right">being here</td><td>being here</td></tr>
</table>

another another
moment moment
I can't stand being here another moment,
as a matter as a matter
of fact of fact
I never I never
want want
to see you to see you
again again
I never want to see
you again
I never want to see you again,
as I said as I said
to you over to you over
the telephone the telephone
as I said to you over the telephone
"I hope "I hope
you have a nice you have a nice
weekend" weekend
I hope you have a nice weekend,"
you're running you're running
on empty on empty
you're running on empty
you're running on empty
and I feel and I feel
old old
and ugly and ugly
and I feel old
and ugly
and I feel old and ugly,
and I don't and I don't
want want
to talk to talk
to anybody to anybody
and I don't want to talk

to anybody
and I don't want to talk to anybody,
nothing   nothing
I've ever   I've ever
loved   loved
nothing I've ever
loved
no matter   no matter
how much   how much
the potential   the potential
nothing I ever loved
no matter how much the potential
was ever   was ever
worth   worth
the suffering   the suffering
was ever worth
the suffering
was ever worth the suffering,
you're on   you're on
United   United
Flight Number   Flight Number
222   222
you're on United Flight Number 222,
I think   I think
we're over   we're over
Kansas   Kansas
I think we're over Kansas
because   because
the earth   the earth
is covered   is covered
with squares   with squares
and rectangles   and rectangles
because the earth
is covered with squares and rectangles,
flying   flying

back back
to New York to New York
flying back to New York,
covered with squares and rectangles,
sipping sipping
a whiskey a whiskey
sipping a whiskey,
flying back to New York,
no matter no matter
how how
famous famous
I become I become
no matter how famous I become,
no matter no matter
how much how much
money money
I make I make
no matter how much money I make,
no matter how no matter how
beautiful beautiful
I used to be I used to be
no matter how beautiful I used to be,
I'm always I'm always
totally totally
lonely lonely
I'm always totally
lonely
I'm always
totally lonely
I'm always totally lonely,
and if I wasn't and if I wasn't
a fucking a fucking
Buddhist Buddhist
and if I wasn't a fucking Buddhist,
I'd love I'd love

to put	to put
a gun	a gun
in my mouth	in my mouth
	I'd love to put
	a gun in my mouth
	I'd love to put a gun in my mouth
and blow	and blow
my fucking	my fucking
head	head
off	off
	and blow my fucking head off
in slow	in slow
motion,	motion,
and the pilot	and the pilot
says	says
we're flying	we're flying
at 37,000	at 37,000
feet	feet
over Kansas	over Kansas
	we're flying at 37,000 feet over Kansas,
wide	wide
open	open
	wide open
blue	blue
	wide open blue
evening	evening
sky,	sky,
grasping	grasping
at emptiness	at emptiness
	grasping at emptiness
	grasping at emptiness,
I keep	I keep
repeating	repeating
this	this
to myself	to myself

	I keep repeating
	this to myself
	I keep repeating this to myself,
	I said
	it to you
	I said it to you,
I remember saying it to you,	I remember saying it to you,
	you get
	you get
	you get
you get	you get
no cover	no cover
from your backdoor	from your backdoor
lover	lover
	you get no cover
	from your backdoor lover,
you're standing	you're standing
at a subway	at a subway
urinal	urinal
	you're standing at a subway urinal,
pulling	pulling
on your meat	on your meat
	pulling on your meat
	pulling on your meat,
cause	cause
I want	I want
to make love	to make love
to somebody	to somebody
on my way	on my way
back	back
downtown	downtown
	cause I want to make love
	to somebody
	on my way back downtown
	cause I want to make love to

somebody
on my way back downtown,
you're standing at a subway urinal,
somebody somebody
is sucking is sucking
your cock your cock
somebody is sucking
your cock
somebody is sucking your cock,
and someone and someone
else else
comes up comes up
next to you next to you
and someone else comes up next to you,
and you're and you're
kissing him kissing him
and you're kissing him
and you're kissing him,
the Howard the Howard
Johnson Johnson
toilet toilet
on the Garden on the Garden
State State
Parkway, Parkway,
the Long Island the Long Island
men's men's
room room
in Freeport, in Freeport,
I saw it I saw it
in a Walt Disney in a Walt Disney
cartoon cartoon
once once
I saw it in a Walt Disney cartoon once,
here here
you're gone you're gone

today   today
here you're gone
today
here you're gone today
and all   and all
I ever   I ever
wanted to do   wanted to do
was to love you   was to love you
and all I wanted to do was
to love you
here you're gone today and all I ever
wanted to do was to love you,
grasping
at emptiness
grasping at emptiness   grasping at emptiness
grasping at emptiness,
I've made
so many
mistakes
in my life
I've made so many mistakes   I've made so many mistakes
in my life   in my life
I've made so many mistakes in my life,
I only got
3 dollars
in my pocket
I only got 3 dollars in my pocket,   I only got 3 dollars in my pocket,
I'm sitting
in a car
on an expressway
in a traffic
jam
I'm sitting in a car on an expressway   I'm sitting in a car on an expressway
in a traffic jam,   in a traffic jam,
I like

<table>
<tr><td align="right">dirty</td><td></td></tr>
<tr><td align="right">sex</td><td></td></tr>
<tr><td align="right">I like</td><td>I like</td></tr>
<tr><td align="right">dirty sex</td><td>dirty sex</td></tr>
<tr><td align="right">I like dirty sex,</td><td></td></tr>
<tr><td align="right">I like it</td><td></td></tr>
<tr><td align="right">when</td><td></td></tr>
<tr><td align="right">you</td><td></td></tr>
<tr><td align="right">cum</td><td></td></tr>
<tr><td align="right">when I'm pissing</td><td></td></tr>
<tr><td align="right">in your mouth</td><td></td></tr>
<tr><td align="right">I like it when you cum</td><td>I like it when you cum</td></tr>
<tr><td align="right">when I'm pissing in your mouth,</td><td>when I'm pissing in your mouth,</td></tr>
<tr><td align="right">and hot</td><td></td></tr>
<tr><td align="right">concrete</td><td></td></tr>
<tr><td align="right">road</td><td></td></tr>
<tr><td align="right">and hot concrete road</td><td>and hot concrete road</td></tr>
<tr><td align="right">and highway</td><td></td></tr>
<tr><td align="right">and highway</td><td>and highway</td></tr>
<tr><td align="right">and overpasses</td><td></td></tr>
<tr><td align="right">popping</td><td></td></tr>
<tr><td align="right">and overpasses popping,</td><td>and overpasses popping,</td></tr>
<tr><td align="right">you haven't got</td><td>you haven't got</td></tr>
<tr><td align="right">anything</td><td>anything</td></tr>
<tr><td align="right">to lose,</td><td>to lose,</td></tr>
<tr><td></td><td>cause</td></tr>
<tr><td></td><td>nothing</td></tr>
<tr><td></td><td>you've ever</td></tr>
<tr><td></td><td>done</td></tr>
<tr><td></td><td>has been any</td></tr>
<tr><td></td><td>good</td></tr>
<tr><td align="right">cause nothing you've ever done</td><td>cause nothing you've ever done</td></tr>
<tr><td align="right">has been any good</td><td>has been any good</td></tr>
<tr><td></td><td>cause nothing you've ever done has been
any good,</td></tr>
</table>

<table>
<tr><td></td><td>big</td></tr>
<tr><td></td><td>ego</td></tr>
<tr><td>big ego</td><td>big ego</td></tr>
<tr><td></td><td>big ego,</td></tr>
<tr><td></td><td>and hustle</td></tr>
<tr><td>and hustle</td><td>and hustle</td></tr>
<tr><td></td><td>and hustle,</td></tr>
<tr><td></td><td>and it's all</td></tr>
<tr><td></td><td>over now,</td></tr>
<tr><td></td><td>baby</td></tr>
<tr><td>it's all over now, baby,</td><td>it's all over now, baby,</td></tr>
<tr><td></td><td>you haven't got anything</td></tr>
<tr><td></td><td>to lose</td></tr>
<tr><td></td><td>you haven't got anything to lose,</td></tr>
<tr><td></td><td>and I don't know</td></tr>
<tr><td></td><td>where</td></tr>
<tr><td></td><td>the money</td></tr>
<tr><td></td><td>comes from</td></tr>
<tr><td>and I don't know where</td><td>and I don't know where</td></tr>
<tr><td>the money comes from</td><td>the money comes from</td></tr>
<tr><td></td><td>and I don't know where the money</td></tr>
<tr><td></td><td>comes from,</td></tr>
<tr><td></td><td>it's all</td></tr>
<tr><td></td><td>going</td></tr>
<tr><td></td><td>to end</td></tr>
<tr><td></td><td>tomorrow</td></tr>
<tr><td>it's all going to end</td><td>it's all going to end</td></tr>
<tr><td>tomorrow</td><td>tomorrow</td></tr>
<tr><td></td><td>it's all going to end tomorrow,</td></tr>
<tr><td></td><td></td></tr>
<tr><td>three</td><td></td></tr>
<tr><td>times</td><td></td></tr>
<tr><td>today</td><td></td></tr>
<tr><td>I dialed</td><td></td></tr>
<tr><td>your number</td><td></td></tr>
<tr><td>three times today</td><td></td></tr>
<tr><td>I dialed your number</td><td></td></tr>
</table>

ree times today I dialed your number,
you weren't
there
you weren't there
you weren't there,
I keep
thinking
about you
I keep thinking
about you
I keep thinking about you,
and I know
you're a reflection
of my mind
and I know you're a reflection
of my mind
nd I know you're a reflection of my mind,
I'm lying
down
here
on my bed
I'm lying down here on my bed,
thinking about
when
I'm going to see you
nking about when I'm going to see you,
I'm going
to say to you
I'm going to say to you
I'm going to say to you,
don't think
too much
tonight,
baby
don't think too much tonight, baby,

three times today I dialed your number,
you weren't there,
I keep thinking about you,
and I know you're a reflection of my mind,
I'm lying down here on my bed,
thinking about when I'm going to see you,
I'm going to say to you,
don't think too much tonight, baby,
spend

	the night
	with me
	spend
	the night with me
spend the night with me,	spend the night with me,
	stay
	until
	the break
	of day
stay until the break of day,	stay until the break of day,
	share
	this night
	with me
share this night with me	share this night with me
	in my arms
	in my arms
in my arms,	in my arms,
	I keep
	looking
	for the feeling
	I lost
	when
	I lost you
	I keep looking for the feeling
	I lost when I lost you
I keep looking for the feeling I lost	I keep looking for the feeling I lost
when I lost you,	when I lost you,
	and it was
	bullshit
	and it was bullshit
and it was bullshit,	and it was bullshit,
	and now,
	baby,
	it's chickenshit
and now, baby, it's chickenshit	and now, baby, it's chickenshit.

<table>
<tr><td></td><td>we're sitting</td></tr>
<tr><td></td><td>on the green</td></tr>
<tr><td></td><td>couch</td></tr>
<tr><td>we're sitting on the green couch,</td><td>we're sitting on the green couch,</td></tr>
<tr><td></td><td>I'm hugging</td></tr>
<tr><td></td><td>you</td></tr>
<tr><td></td><td>I'm hugging you</td></tr>
<tr><td>I'm hugging you,</td><td>I'm hugging you,</td></tr>
<tr><td></td><td>we're kissing</td></tr>
<tr><td>we're kissing,</td><td>we're kissing,</td></tr>
<tr><td></td><td>I wish</td></tr>
<tr><td></td><td>I knew</td></tr>
<tr><td></td><td>how</td></tr>
<tr><td></td><td>to make</td></tr>
<tr><td></td><td>love</td></tr>
<tr><td></td><td>to you</td></tr>
<tr><td></td><td>I wish I knew how</td></tr>
<tr><td></td><td>to make love to you</td></tr>
<tr><td>I wish I knew how to make love to you,</td><td>I wish I knew how to make love to you,</td></tr>
<tr><td></td><td>when</td></tr>
<tr><td></td><td>I was in</td></tr>
<tr><td></td><td>Rome,</td></tr>
<tr><td></td><td>Italy</td></tr>
<tr><td>when I was in Rome, Italy,</td><td>when I was in Rome, Italy,</td></tr>
<tr><td>fettucini</td><td>fettucini</td></tr>
<tr><td>alfredo,</td><td>alfredo,</td></tr>
<tr><td></td><td>Marion</td></tr>
<tr><td></td><td>Javits</td></tr>
<tr><td></td><td>give me</td></tr>
<tr><td></td><td>another</td></tr>
<tr><td></td><td>hit</td></tr>
<tr><td></td><td>of the popper</td></tr>
<tr><td>Marion Javits give me another</td><td>Marion Javits give me another</td></tr>
<tr><td>hit of the popper,</td><td>hit of the popper,</td></tr>
<tr><td>you're not</td><td>you're not</td></tr>
</table>

going	going
to find	to find
what you	what you
want	want
in this bar	in this bar
	you're not going to find
	what you want in this bar
	you're not going to find what you want
	in this bar,
you know	you know
you're not	you're not
going to	going to
find him	find him
anywhere	anywhere
	and you know you're not going
	to find him anywhere
	you know you're not going to find him
	anywhere,
you're cruising	you're cruising
the baths	the baths
	you're cruising the baths
	you're cruising the baths,
looking in	looking in
the dimly	the dimly
lit	lit
rooms	rooms
	looking in the dimly lit rooms,
these guys	these guys
posing	posing
for pornographic	for pornographic
pictures	pictures
	these guys looking like
	they're posing for pornographic pictures
I want	I want
to make it	to make it

with you	with you
I want to make	
it with you	
I want to make	
it with you	
I want to make it	
with you	
I want to make it with you,	
the guy	the guy
in a Levi	in a Levi
shirt	shirt
with a hard on	with a hard on
the guy in a Levi shirt with a hard on,	
you're walking	you're walking
down	down
7th Avenue	7th Avenue
you're walking down 7th Avenue,	
and all	and all
these people	these people
are passing you	are passing you
and all these people	
are passing you	
and all these people are passing you,	
everyone	
of them	
has a lover	
everyone of them has a lover,	everyone of them has a lover,
and how	and how
come	come
I'm alone	I'm alone
	and how come
	I'm alone
	and how come I'm alone,
we're in	we're in
your room	your room

<table>
<tr><td align="right">and we’re kissing</td><td>and we’re kissing</td></tr>
<tr><td></td><td>we’re in your room and we’re kissing.</td></tr>
<tr><td></td><td>we’re holding</td></tr>
<tr><td></td><td>you tight</td></tr>
<tr><td></td><td>we’re holding you tight,</td></tr>
<tr><td align="right">and there may be</td><td>and there may be</td></tr>
<tr><td align="right">no</td><td>no</td></tr>
<tr><td align="right">attachment</td><td>attachment</td></tr>
<tr><td align="right">to the object</td><td>to the object</td></tr>
<tr><td align="right">of grasping</td><td>of grasping</td></tr>
<tr><td align="right">and there may be no attachment</td><td></td></tr>
<tr><td align="right">to the object of grasping,</td><td></td></tr>
<tr><td align="right">but it’s attachment</td><td>but it’s attachment</td></tr>
<tr><td align="right">to grasping</td><td>to grasping</td></tr>
<tr><td align="right">but it’s attachment to grasping,</td><td>but it’s attachment to grasping,</td></tr>
<tr><td align="right">all you</td><td></td></tr>
<tr><td align="right">got to do</td><td></td></tr>
<tr><td align="right">is look at it</td><td></td></tr>
<tr><td align="right">all you got to do is look at it,</td><td>all you got to do is look at it,</td></tr>
<tr><td></td><td>a hologram</td></tr>
<tr><td></td><td>in my heart</td></tr>
<tr><td align="right">a hologram in my heart,</td><td>a hologram in my heart,</td></tr>
<tr><td align="right">and dissolve it</td><td>and dissolve it</td></tr>
<tr><td></td><td>and dissolve it</td></tr>
<tr><td></td><td>and dissolve,</td></tr>
<tr><td align="right">and pull</td><td>and pull</td></tr>
<tr><td align="right">the plug,</td><td>the plug,</td></tr>
<tr><td></td><td>turn</td></tr>
<tr><td></td><td>the TV</td></tr>
<tr><td></td><td>off</td></tr>
<tr><td align="right">turn the TV off,</td><td>turn the TV off,</td></tr>
<tr><td align="right">is what</td><td>is what</td></tr>
<tr><td align="right">turns</td><td>turns</td></tr>
<tr><td align="right">into bliss</td><td>into bliss</td></tr>
<tr><td align="right">is what turns</td><td>is what turns</td></tr>
</table>

<table>
<tr><td align="right">into bliss</td><td>into bliss</td></tr>
<tr><td align="right">is what turns into bliss,</td><td>is what turns into bliss,</td></tr>
<tr><td align="right">dissolving</td><td>dissolving</td></tr>
<tr><td align="right">desire</td><td>desire</td></tr>
<tr><td align="right">dissolving desire</td><td>dissolving desire</td></tr>
<tr><td align="right">dissolving desire</td><td>dissolving desire</td></tr>
<tr><td align="right">becomes</td><td>becomes</td></tr>
<tr><td align="right">bliss</td><td>bliss</td></tr>
<tr><td align="right">becomes bliss</td><td>becomes bliss</td></tr>
<tr><td align="right">becomes bliss,</td><td>becomes bliss,</td></tr>
<tr><td align="right">pure</td><td>pure</td></tr>
<tr><td align="right">phenomena</td><td>phenomena</td></tr>
<tr><td align="right">pure phenomena</td><td>pure phenomena</td></tr>
<tr><td align="right">pure phenomena,</td><td>pure phenomena,</td></tr>
<tr><td align="right">not</td><td>not</td></tr>
<tr><td align="right">thinking</td><td>thinking</td></tr>
<tr><td align="right">about it</td><td>about it</td></tr>
<tr><td align="right">not thinking</td><td>not thinking</td></tr>
<tr><td align="right">about it</td><td>about it</td></tr>
<tr><td align="right">not thinking about it,</td><td>not thinking about it,</td></tr>
<tr><td align="right">taking it</td><td>taking it</td></tr>
<tr><td align="right">easy</td><td>easy</td></tr>
<tr><td align="right">taking it easy</td><td>taking it easy</td></tr>
<tr><td align="right">taking it easy,</td><td>taking it easy,</td></tr>
<tr><td align="right">confidence,</td><td>confidence,</td></tr>
<tr><td align="right">fearlessness</td><td>fearlessness</td></tr>
<tr><td align="right">and tranquility</td><td>and tranquility</td></tr>
<tr><td align="right">confidence, fearlessness and tranquility,</td><td>confidence, fearlessness and tranquility,</td></tr>
<tr><td></td><td>pure</td></tr>
<tr><td></td><td>empty</td></tr>
<tr><td></td><td>phenomena,</td></tr>
<tr><td align="right">but after</td><td></td></tr>
<tr><td align="right">all</td><td></td></tr>
<tr><td align="right">these long</td><td></td></tr>
<tr><td align="right">years</td><td></td></tr>
</table>

<table>
<tr><td align="right">but after all these long years,</td><td>but after all these long years,</td></tr>
<tr><td align="right">my meditation</td><td></td></tr>
<tr><td align="right">isn’t so</td><td></td></tr>
<tr><td align="right">good</td><td></td></tr>
<tr><td align="right">my meditation isn’t so good,</td><td>my meditation isn’t so good,</td></tr>
<tr><td align="right">the guy</td><td></td></tr>
<tr><td align="right">on the 2nd</td><td></td></tr>
<tr><td align="right">floor</td><td></td></tr>
<tr><td align="right">the guy on the 2nd floor</td><td></td></tr>
<tr><td align="right">is mostly</td><td></td></tr>
<tr><td align="right">stoned</td><td></td></tr>
<tr><td align="right">on grass</td><td></td></tr>
<tr><td align="right">is mostly stoned on grass,</td><td>is mostly stoned on grass,</td></tr>
<tr><td align="right">listening</td><td>listening</td></tr>
<tr><td align="right">to disco</td><td>to disco</td></tr>
<tr><td align="right">listening to disco</td><td></td></tr>
<tr><td align="right">listening to disco,</td><td></td></tr>
<tr><td align="right">ain’t no</td><td></td></tr>
<tr><td align="right">way</td><td></td></tr>
<tr><td align="right">I can</td><td></td></tr>
<tr><td align="right">live</td><td></td></tr>
<tr><td align="right">without you</td><td></td></tr>
<tr><td align="right">ain’t no way</td><td>ain’t no way</td></tr>
<tr><td align="right">I can live without you</td><td>I can live without you</td></tr>
<tr><td align="right">ain’t no way I can live without you,</td><td></td></tr>
<tr><td align="right">standing</td><td>standing</td></tr>
<tr><td align="right">right</td><td>right</td></tr>
<tr><td align="right">here</td><td>here</td></tr>
<tr><td align="right">standing right here,</td><td></td></tr>
<tr><td align="right">waiting</td><td>waiting</td></tr>
<tr><td align="right">on your return</td><td>on your return</td></tr>
<tr><td align="right">waiting on your return</td><td></td></tr>
<tr><td align="right">waiting on your return,</td><td></td></tr>
<tr><td align="right"></td><td>I just</td></tr>
<tr><td align="right"></td><td>love</td></tr>
</table>

to turn
the FM
radio
to dancing
music
I just love to turn the FM radio   I just love to turn the FM radio
to dancing music,   to dancing music,
get stoned
get stoned   get stoned
get stoned,
sip
some vodka
sip some vodka   sip some vodka
and think
and think
and think
and think
and think

(1978)

LIFE IS A KILLER

Everyone says
what they do
is right,
and money is
a good
thing
it can be
wonderful.

Road
drinking,
driving
around
drinking
beer,
they need me
more than
I need them,
where are
you guys from,
stumbling off
into the night
thinking
about it.

When I was
15 years old,
I knew
everything
there was
to know,
and now that

I'm old,
it was true.

I got dragged
along on
this one
by my foot,
if I wasn't so
tired
I would have
a good
time
if I wasn't so tired
I'd have a good time
if I wasn't so tired I'd have
a good time.

Tossing
and turning,
cause there's
a nest
of wasps
coursing
through your
bloodstream
cause there's a nest of wasps
coursing through your bloodstream.

If you think
about it
how could
it have come
to this
if you think about it
how could it have come to this,

it's coming
down the road,
right through
the red
lights,
and it's
there
and it's there
and it's there
and it's there.

Try your
best
and think
you're good,
that's what
I want
being inside you
that's what I want
being inside you
that's what I want being inside you,
endless
threshold,
and you hope
you're doing
it right.

How are you
feeling good
how are you
feeling
good
how are
you feeling good
how are you feeling

good
how are you feeling good,
you need
national
attention.

Cause essentially
all you
ever accomplished
was snort
some smack
and sit
on a zafu
watching
your breath.

How the hell
did I end
up
doing this
for a job?

I can't say
I don't need
anybody,
cause I need
the Buddhas,
and there's
nothing
I can say
about them.

Everyone is at
a complete
disadvantage,

you're being taken
to dinner
at La Cote Basque
and you're eating
9 Lives
liver
and drinking
wine,
the women
are taking
prisoners,
I'm not going
nowhere,
I ripped up
my suitcases
I ripped up my suitcases.

Crank me
up
and keep me
open
crank me up
and keep me open,
crank me up and keep me open,
nothing
recedes
like success.

Whatever
happens
it will seem
the way
it seems
now,
and it doesn't matter

what you
feel,
how perfectly
correct
or amazing
the clarity,
everything
you think
is deluded
everything you think
is deluded
everything you think is deluded,
life
is a killer.

(1982)

I RESIGNED MYSELF TO BEING HERE

Instructions for reading this poem: each stanza should be read in one breath.

You're backed
up
in a dark
corner
and you don't
know
who's
hitting you
you're backed up in a dark corner
and you don't know who's hitting you,

and I'm sitting
all
by myself
inside
a taxi,
driving
down
Lexington
at 34th,
waiting
to get
downtown
waiting to get
downtown
waiting
to get downtown
waiting to get downtown,

you're heavy
and angry
and depressed
you're heavy and angry and depressed,
you've been
around
for a long
time
you've been around for a long time,

I always
live
with a woman.
I never
live
with a man,
and I make it
with men
and I make it with men
and I make it with men,
and they know
how to
love you,
and I make
my women
go to work
and give me
money,
sorry,
I go
with a guy
only
one
time,

and you're making
drinks
for animals
and hungry
ghosts
and you're making drinks
for animals and hungry ghosts,
you're cooking
dinner
in a hell
world,
you're not
human
you're making
believe
you're human,
sitting
here
in this chair,

I'm walking
around
this party
with a drink
in my hand,
give me
just
a little
more
time
and our love
will surely
grow
give me just a little more time
and our love will surely grow,

beer
stink,
cigarette
smoke,
and music,
walking
to the bar
toilet,
you're the
only one
you're the only
one
you're the only one,
to take me
back
to where
we started
from,
so fill me
up
to the top,
don't you
stop
until I'm
overflowing,

and now
you're in
some American
re-incarnation,
and besides
not remembering
you're talking,
you're telling me
this story,

and not
only
can't I
concentrate
on your words
or understand
what you're
talking
about,
I can't
stand
the incessant
sound
of ignorance
in your voice,
and sleeping
next
to you
is like sleeping
next to
somebody
on the subway
and sleeping next to you
is like sleeping next to
somebody on the subway,
send her
back
home
to Brooklyn,
you gotta
get her
out of
the way,

and it's 5
in the morning,
you're stoned
and wired,
cruising
the sidewalk
cruising the sidewalk,
and I'm not
tired
yet
and I'm not
tired yet
and I'm not tired yet,
cocaine
and I'm alone,
and you're not
going
home
until you
do it
again
and you're not going home
until you do it again
and you're not going home until
you do it again,

uncertain,
and I'm sorry,
but I'm holding
on to
what
I want
I'm holding on to what I want
is right,

caught up
in wanting,
and letting it
go,

sugar,
alcohol,
meat,
heroin,
and cigarettes,
sugar, alcohol, meat,
heroin, and cigarettes,
sugar, alcohol, meat, heroin, and cigarettes
I resigned
myself
to being
here,

your face
is puffed
and grey,
booze
and dope,
fat
and wrinkles,
and I'm
thinking
again
about
what
happened
today
and I'm thinking again
about what happened today,

when
you're with
a lot
of people
you gotta
keep
talking
and when
you're by
yourself
you gotta
keep moving
your hands,

you're in
some fake
category,
you created
for yourself,
so that's
what
happened
to the kid,
I just
want to
thank you
for a wonderful
time,

and you're not
gonna fall
down
cause you're
drunk
and you're not gonna fall down
cause you're drunk,

or nod
out
walking
cause
you're stoned,

and I made
one
big
mistake
tonight
and I made one big mistake tonight,

the bar
is closing
and there's
something
you dislike
about
everyone
in this room
and there's something you dislike
about everyone in this room,
but I'm
gonna
do it
one more
time,
too much
is not
enough,

you're my
toilet,
eat it
out,

I'm gonna
feed you
you're my toilet,
eat it out,
I'm gonna feed you,
you're my toilet, eat it out,
I'm gonna feed you,

and it's
the 1980s
and I can't
believe
I survived
the 1970s
as awful
as they were,
and if you're
gonna
judge me,
don't
judge me,
lightly,
the politics
make it
completely
discouraging
the politics make it
completely discouraging,
and all
I want
now
is money
and all I want now
is money
and all I want now is money,

Buddha
Mind,
what
happened?

and all
I got to
say is,
I'll see you
in another
life
I'll see you in another life,
doubtless
I will,
and I can
wait,

The Chicago
Conspiracy
and you were in
some filthy
jail
cause they
pulled
the wool
over your eyes
about some
dumb ass
anti-Vietnamese
War,
and in 1970,
I couldn't
believe
I survived
the 1960s,

and in 1970
I couldn't believe I survived the 1960s,
cause I
remember
jumping
off
the Empire
State
Building
with Lucy
in your eyes
like diamonds,
forever,
and you landed
on the concrete
sidewalk
on 34th Street
in an Andy Warhol
picture
in 1963
now selling
for $80,000,

you were dead
in a hospital
bed,
and you get
up
and do it
again
and you get up
and do it again
and you get up and do it
again
and you get up and do it again,

I really
like being
with ya
I really like being with ya,
but I'm
only with you
for what
you can
do for me,
and never
forgetting it
is how
I endure you,
cause you
can't always
get what
you want
cause you can't always
get what you want,
but if you
try sometimes,
you always
get what
you need,

and I know
I'm living
with you
and you're rich
and famous
and I know I'm living with you
and you're rich and famous,
but I ain't
here
for any
love affair

but I ain't here
for any love affair
but I ain't here for any love affair,
and as you know
I have a
batting
average,
you've had
the best,
and besides
their reputations
and media
visibility,
they weren't
altogether
that good,
just
like me,

and I pay
myself
the big
bills,
I own
this
place
I own
this place
I own this place,
but I'm
leaving
cause I
had enough
but I'm leaving cause
I've had enough,

you're laying
in bed
playing
with your meat,
waiting
to go to
sleep
after somebody
you just
made it with
went home
you're laying in bed
playing with your meat,
waiting to go to sleep
after somebody you just
made it with went home,

good
morning
America,
how
are ya;
and my friend
got me
some good
clean
junk
and my friend got me
some good clean junk,
and he got it
from his friend
In Brooklyn
2 days
ago,

and that guy
gets it
for himself,
you weren't
a suicide
against
your best
wishes,
and you didn't
burn out,
or get
enlightened,
and I don't
feel like
standing
here
reading
a poem
to you
and I don't feel like standing here
reading a poem to you,
dragging
concrete,
it's like
having a lead
weight
in your heart,

and we've stayed
together
for 15
years
only
cause
we've never

stopped
fighting,
you've got
no other
place
to go,
and you know
what
it's like
waiting
for the bus,
I don't
know
why
I've faithfully
gone on
working
for you,
and I don't know why
I've gone on
servicing you,
cause
everyone
I know
who's done it
is a jerk,

you don't
even
pay
any money
you don't even
pay any money
you don't even pay any money,
and I'm tired

of your disapproval
and I'm tired of your disapproval,

making
love to you
is looking
in a bathroom
mirror,
and I keep
asking
for it
and I keep
asking for it
and I keep asking for it
and I keep asking for it,

and both
of us
standing
there
as empty
as each
other,

and I just
fell
asleep
for 2
hours
in the afternoon
and I just fell asleep
for 2 hours in the afternoon,
I was
eating

honey
and then I
licked it
off
my fingers,

you've been
in the front
line
for a long
time
you've been in the front line for a long time,
from the beginning,
not to
talk
about
the cross-fire,
you've been
hit
so many
times,
give me
a break,
and I like
my wounds
licked
and I like my wounds
licked,

you're the way
I like to
do it
you're the way
I like to do it,
whip

your ass
whip your ass,
and every time
I slap
your face
you kiss me,
and it sure
feels
good
holding
ya
and it sure feels good
holding ya,
you know
how
to love me
you know how
to love me
you know how to
love me
you know how to love me,

dreaming
I was
dreaming
dreaming I
was dreaming
dreaming I was dreaming,
like getting
to an itch
you've been trying
to get to
for weeks,
I said
I would

do it
I said I
would do it
I said I would do it,
I told you
I could
do it,
take me
home,
lots
of luck
and now
I'm going
to say
goodbye.

(1980)

STRETCHING IT WIDER

Some things
that work
in one
decade,
don't work
in the next,
so mark
it down
as a noble
idea
that failed.

And I did
what everybody
dreams
of doing,
I walked
away
from it
I walked away
from it
I walked away from it
I walked away from it,
and I never
went back,
without reconcile.

And since I
can't leave,
I love
getting drunk
with you

from YOU GOT TO BURN TO SHINE, 1994

I love getting
drunk with you
I love getting drunk with you,
and give me some
more blow.

Nobody
ever gives
you what
you want
except by mistake,
and the only
things you
ever got
is what
you did for yourself,
cause you
hate them
and you're only
doing it
everyday
for the money,
you hate them
and you're only doing it
everyday for the money.

I know guys
who work
all their
life
and have got
a lot,
and something
happens to him,
and he loses

everything
just like that,
and I haven't
even got
that
and I haven't even got that.

Hard
work,
low
pay,
and embarrassing
conditions,
you are worse
than I remember,
and you're
home
and you're home
and you're home
and you're home
and you're home.

What is
a rat doing,
when it
isn't eating
garbage
or scaring you
on the street,
they're laying
around
like pussy cats,
you and I
sleeping in
the bed sheets,

warm
and cozy,
sliding
your legs
under the covers
and staying there.

You got to keep
down
cause they're shooting
low,
press your body
against the ground,
it's gravity,
the telephone
hasn't rung
once today.

If there is
one thing
you cannot
and will not
do
is make
this world
a better
place,
if there's one thing
you can't do
is make the world
a better place,
if there's one thing
you're not going to do
is make the world a better place.

Cause you are
only successful
when you
rip
somebody off,
and everybody
I've ever known
who wants to
help somebody,
wants to
help themselves
and I'm a firm
believer in
giving somebody
enough rope
to hang themselves.

You're standing here
watching all
these people,
and everything seems
a little
confused
and everything seems
a little confused,
I haven't got
anything to say.

The noose
is tightening
the noose is tightening
the noose is tightening,
and let me make
one more
further

observation,
when you
die,
you're going to die
with a hard-on.

If I didn't
have an
accident
I wouldn't
be here
If I didn't have
an accident
I wouldn't be here
If I didn't have an accident
I wouldn't be here.

Then there is
the reality
of the family,
your mother
and father,
them and
my mistakes
is why
I'm sitting
at a table
with a bunch
of stupid
jerks
on Thanksgiving
eating
a turkey
stuffed
with lasagna.

I'm spending
my whole
life
being with
people
I don't want
to be with
I'm spending my whole
life being with people
I don't want to be with
I'm spending my whole life
being with people
I don't want to be with,
and there ain't
no such thing
as family,
just people
you work with.

I love
completely
perverted
people,
you are my
best
sexual
fantasy,

I never got
that far with
scat
before
and I want to
remember it,

tireless
and I want to remember it,
tireless
and I want to remember it, tireless.

We make money
the old-fashioned
way,
we earn it,
the anchor
man
never leaves
the building,
and the only
difference
between me
and a preacher,
is he's
telling you
he has a way
out,
and I'm telling you
don't bother,
for you
there is
no way
out
for you there
is no way out
for you there is no
way out
for you there is no way out,
and it isn't
as though
you got anything
to lose.

Besides they
blocked
permanently
all
the exits
they blocked permanently
all the exits,
you and I
get to
stay here
forever
and it gets
worse
beyond your
imagination.

I would like
to give my
best
to all sentient
beings,
and before
I die,
I'd like
to de-tox
my mind
and tame
delusion,
but we are not
in a time
appropriate
to do this.

Tonight,
I want you
to give us
some drugs
and a little
alcohol,
if something
is good
people
like it
if something is good
people like it
if something is good people like it.

It looks
the way
it should
and you make me
feel good,
so let's
open it
up,
stretching it
wider
stretching
it wider
stretching it wider
stretching it wider
stretching it
wider,
and it shouldn't be
any trouble.

(1982)

EXILED IN DOMESTIC LIFE

I'm standing
in the hall,
I pushed
the button,
and I'm waiting
for the elevator,
you are alone
and you are unstable
and you're not sure
it's OK
anymore,
exiled
in domestic
life
exiled in
domestic life
exiled in domestic life.

Nobody does
it for you,
you got to
do it
all by yourself,
and I've been
brutalized
and I've been brutalized
and I've been brutalized
and I've been brutalized.

from YOU GOT TO BURN TO SHINE, 1994

I would rather
be dead,
than 18 years old,
and a poet,
and if I can
do that,
I can sit
on somebody's
face
I can sit on
somebody's face
I can sit on somebody's face,
and feed.

I want to
sleep
hugging
someone
over and
over again
I want to sleep hugging
someone over and over
again,
and cuddling
in the morning,
cause it's
healing
my body
in my heart,
it's safe
to be married
these days
it's safe to be married
these days.

When you got
lots of negative
thoughts,
they are big,
and powerful
and wonderful
they are big, and powerful
and wonderful
they are big,
and powerful and wonderful,
it's their
job
to get it up,
it's not
your problem.

If it isn't
black,
it's not
good,
and it's not going
to work,
you don't feel
a razor
blade
you don't feel a razor blade,
and I like juice,
your skin
smells like
an old sponge
soaked in
alcohol,
and this place
stinks.

from **YOU GOT TO BURN TO SHINE, 1994**

A hundred
million
years ago,
the geophysical
adjustments
that made petroleum
from primordial
forests,
maybe 100 million
years from now,
will transform
the plastic
in our garbage
into something
better than
diamonds.

The reason
it's good,
is cause
I work
all the time,
and I've been spending
the rest
of my time,
laying on
the bed
with my girlfriend
watching TV,
and I want her
to tell me
wisdom
when she doesn't
know she is
and I want her to tell

me wisdom
when she doesn't know
she is
and I want her to tell me
wisdom when
she doesn't know she is.

What are you
slapping your
hands
together for,
do you want
me to slap
your face?

(1983)

IT'S A MISTAKE TO THINK YOU'RE SPECIAL

You sit
there
thinking about
the things
you said
over and
over again,
and I just want
to sit
here
and think,
cause it's
powerful.

I love
being where
people
like
being with
each other,
and then I want to take
the night off,
something soft
and protective,
I want to stay
asleep
for as long
as I can
I want to stay
asleep
for as long

as I can
I want to stay
asleep for
as long as I can
I want to stay asleep
for as long as I can,

you have to be
ruthless
and accepting
with nightmares.

They convinced me
I was wrong,
and I believed them,
and you will never
be able to
forgive them,

unbuilding
a building
stone
by stone
unbuilding a building
stone by stone
unbuilding a building stone
by stone,
going backwards

everyone I know
is just like me,
they're stupid.

Tell me what
I should do,

but please
tell it to me
while I'm sleeping
so I'll remember,
the walls inside
my house are made
of human skulls
fitted together
like bricks,
and the floor
I'm standing on
is soaked
with blood
and bile.

OK, where are
the warrior
priests,
we need
retributions
warrior priests
we need retribution,

offering
death
for a reason
to make something
happen,

straight,
or with alcohol,
drugs and
sexual
energy,

there is leverage
in wealth,
feeding
the hole
feeding the hole
feeding the hole
feeding the hole
feeding the hole,
spit in it,
spit here.

Butterflies
sucking
on the carcass
of a dead bird,
and your body
is being pulled down
backwards
into the world
below,
as a king.

I feel most
at home
among the defiled
I feel most at
home among
the defiled
I feel most at home among
the defiled,
in the center
of a flower
under a deep
blue
sky,

it's a mistake
to think
you're special.

(1984)

BERLIN & CHERNOBYL

William Burroughs and I
were in Berlin
the week after
Chernobyl,
and we got caught
endlessly
in the warm
Spring
rains,
big
fat
raindrops
filled with
radioactivity,
splashing in
my face
and running down
my hair
into my lips
over
and over
again,
radioactive
rain
soaked into
William Burroughs'
grey
fedora,
a tiara
of black
diamonds,

from **YOU GOT TO BURN TO SHINE, 1994**

as we ran down
the streets
to the hotel,
big fat
raindrops
bejeweled
with radioactivity
soaked into
this black
leather
jacket
that I'm wearing
tonight,
great
wet
clusters
in the soft
black leather
shoulders,
100,000 ryms,
I only wear it
on special
occasions,
I feel like
Louis the 14th,
I got a coat
sewn with
10,000 diamonds,
and I got off
easy.

(1986)

HI RISQUE

I want
to scat
in your mouth,
I want you
to scat
in my mouth,
I want to scat
on your face
and rub it in

chocolate,
caviar,
and champagne,
absolute
preliminaries

pushing
the inner
envelope
to the limit,
one more
time,
mining
diamonds
with your tongue
for the crown
of one
of the kings
of hell,
when the going
gets rough
the tough
get gorgeous

from **YOU GOT TO BURN TO SHINE, 1994**

squeezing
money
from the air,
snake
tongue,
stretching
your tongue
to the Buddhas

diving
into the wreck
diving into
the wreck
diving into the wreck,
curiosity
and compassion,
and an exercise
in non-aversion,
fear
spiraling
from you
fear spiraling from you,
that gun's got
blood
in its hole

We do not do
this anymore,
but I still
think about it
when I'm
jerking off,

I was king
of promiscuity,
LSD,
crystal meth,
fist fucking
with 40 guys
for 14 hours,
it's worse
than I thought
and now,
every one
of them
I ever made
love to,
every single
one,
is dead,
and may they be
resting
in *great*
equanimity

We gave
a party
for the gods
and the gods
all came.

(1990)

JUST SAY NO TO FAMILY VALUES

On a day when
you're walking
down the street
and you see
a hearse
with a coffin,
followed by
a flower car
and limos,
you know the day
is auspicious,
your plans are going to be
successful;
but on a day when
you see a bride and groom
and wedding party,
watch out,
be careful,
it might be a bad sign.

Just say no
to family values,
and don't quit
your day job.

Drugs
are sacred
substances,
and some drugs
are very sacred substances,

please praise them
for somewhat liberating
the mind.

Tobacco
is a sacred substance
to some,
and even though you've
stopped smoking,
show a little respect.

Alcohol
is totally great,
let us celebrate
the glorious qualities
of booze,
and I had
a good time
being with you.

Just
do it,
just do it
just don't
not do it,
do it.

Christian
Fundamentalists,
and fundamentalists
in general,
are viruses,
and they're killing us,
multiplying
and mutating,

and they're destroying us,
now, you know,
you got to give
strong medicine
to combat
a virus.

Who's buying?
good acid,
I'm flying,
slipping
and sliding,
slurping
and slamming,
I'm sinking,
dipping
and dripping,
and squirting
inside you;
never
fast forward
a come shot;

milk, milk,
lemonade,
round the corner
where the chocolate's made;
I love to see
your face
when you're suffering.

Do it
with anybody
you want,
whatever

you want,
for as long as you want,
any time,
any place,
when it's possible,
and try to be
safe;
in a situation where
you must abandon
yourself
completely
beyond all concepts.

Just say no
to family
values,
we don't have to say no
to family values,
cause we never
think about them;
just
do it,
just make
love
and compassion.

(1994)

EVERYONE GETS LIGHTER

Life is lots of presents,
and every single day you get
a big bunch of gifts
under a sparkling pine tree
hung with countless balls of colored lights,
piles of presents wrapped in fancy paper,
the red box with the green ribbon,
and the green box with the red ribbon,
and the blue one with silver,
and the white one with gold.

It's not
what happens,
it's how you
handle it.

You are in a water bubble human body,
on a private jet
in seemingly a god world,
a glass of champagne,
and a certain luminosity
and emptiness,
skin of air,
a flat sea of white clouds below
and vast dome of blue sky above,
and your mind is an iron nail in-between.

It's not
what happens,
it's how you
handle it.

Dead cat bounce,
catch
the falling knife,
after endless shadow boxing
in your sleep,
fighting in your dreams
and knocking yourself out,
you realize everything is empty,
and appears as miraculous display,
all are in nature
the play of emptiness and clarity.

Everyone
gets
lighter
everyone
gets lighter
everyone gets
lighter
everyone gets lighter,
everyone is light.

(2002)

DOWN COMES THE RAIN

We welcome rain, who want to stay at home,
when angels move, it rains,
the offering that rain spirits in tropical rain forests like best
is chocolate,
and like it as burning chocolate candles.

I want it to rain
for the rest of my life,
I want it to pour rain
to the end of time,
I want the sun never to come out,
let it rain,
rain pinging circles in water,
rain hitting cement and jumping,
rain plucking sound from the earth,
rain fell
down
rain fell down
rain fell down
rain fell down,
water coming through,
sloshing, rushing and rolling down the street,
sweating cold water,
I want it to never stop,
waiting for the next burst of storm,
down
comes
the rain
down comes
the rain
down comes the rain
down comes the rain.

I dive down into sleep,
without dreams,
and sleep forever,
dullness uninhibited,
sinking slowly out,
snuggling my head and heart
on a cushion of emptiness and bliss,
sea water and salty sweet waves crashing and white foam
are white silk scarves
pulling down into the underworld,
holding onto a white umbrella,
descending on cross-current riptides
and an undertow of oblivion,
and I come to rest
with eight naga kings
sitting around me in a circle
wishing me welcome.

The great naga kings
living at the bottom of the seas
are the richest beings in the world,
have greater wealth than any man or god,
they live in palaces below the deepest oceans
and are surrounded by vast treasures
obtained from many worlds and invisible realms,
the upper half of their bodies are human,
and below the waist are huge snakes
and at the end a fish tail,
thick, satin skin, snake kings crowned with fabulous jewels,
and their wives are called nagini queens,
naked from the navel up with big breasts
draped with many strings of pearls
and necklaces of rubies the size of chicken eggs,
seaweed is braided in their hair,
from their hips coils of velvety serpents

fan out on lapis lazuli and jade thrones
in ornate rooms carved into the black basalt bedrock,
subterranean molten lava
and hydrothermal vents
feed their life,
scalding smokers
and boiling hot springs,
they breath through gills
absorbing oxygen from the plankton,
the naga kings, behind their heads, have snake hoods
denoting their rank,
nine hoods is the highest and seven a little lower,
the folds pulled back like the thick foreskin of a dick,
their sky is black,
and their vast darkness
is lit by lights in lamps inside their bodies
called flesh lamps.

I want it to rain
for the rest of my life,
I want it to pour rain
to the end of time,
I want the sun never to come out,
let's rain,
singing
in the rain
singing in the rain,
soaking in the rain,
singing in the rain
singing in the rain
singing in the rain
singing in the rain,
when you ain't got nothing,
you ain't got nothing to lose.

The naga kings and queens are encircled
by retinues of secretaries and servants,
who look soft and easy, but are tricky and cunning,
and the security guards belch poisonous gas
and are known for their strong jaws,
they bite never releasing their grip, like crocodiles,
they live at the bottom of seas
but they have second homes all over the world,
weekend houses like we do,
they can change their bodily forms
as they have miraculous powers,
not to frighten people
with human tops, snake bottoms and the fish tail,
it is their life
and they like it,
in between heaven and earth.

The nagas believe their greatest treasures
are books,
particularly one poem of one hundred thousand stanzas in
twelve volumes,
written in beautiful calligraphy with gold ink
on sapphire blue glassine pages
are stored in crystal reliquary libraries,
the nagas have exuberant devotion to the books,
treating them as objects of veneration,
dancing and swimming,
spinning circles and spiraling around them in the water.

I want it to rain
for the rest of my life,
I want it to pour rain
to the end of time,
I want the sun never to come out,
let it rain,

rain hum
rain hums
rain humming
hung,
turquoise tile and steamy water spraying on warm skin,
in the laughing screams of children playing
are hidden the weeping cries to come,
I am collecting all the tears
I have cried
in every past life
and I am making a vast ocean,
water weeping with joy
wind weeping with appreciation,
heavier than heaven.

Eight naga kings sit around me in a circle,
and from their heart centers
ropes of light
connect to one hundred thousand nagas and naginis
clustered around them,
blazing splendor,
and their vibrations of sound,
similar to the sonar songs of whales,
are really loud resonating syllables
blasting like a rock and roll concert,
seeing the essence of emptiness
and singing beyond conceptualizations,
intrinsic awareness,
imperturbable mind.

Garden fountain water
splashing mindlessly,
water coming out
and dripping down
jiggling endlessly,

water weaving currents,
nets of eddying thoughts,
water deepens
where it waits,
spiraling deep into the underworld,
the wish-fulfilling jewel
can only be obtained by stealing water,
the water thief,
in the sound of water is the singing
of wisdom women water goddesses.

Rainbow kisses
radiating out
filling the universe,
in a bowl of cold water
are atoms
hotter than the surface of a star,
down
comes
the rain
down
comes the rain
down comes the rain
down comes the rain.

(2005)

THERE WAS A BAD TREE

There was a bad
tree
a bad tree,
that people
hated.
The leaves gave off
a foul
smell,
and the flowers
had a bitter
stink.
If you got too close,
you vomited.
The fruit
was poison,
one bite
and you were dead.

Everyone really
disliked it.
The bad tree
stank.
They talked
endlessly about it;
and decided
to cut it down.
Get rid of it.
They chopped
with axes,
and barely made a dent;
wearing breathing masks,
they whacked at it

and whacked at it,
and nibbled and chipped.
Oily powder
from the shiny dark green leaves
got on their skin,
blistered,
and was really itchy;
and they scratched
bloody red.

They put on
protective gear
with oxygen,
and went at it with
electric buzz saws
and heavy equipment.
Working 24-hour shifts,
finally, they cut it down.

Everyone was very happy,
and celebrated
the great victory.
A noble deed, well done;
and they went to bed exhausted.
The next morning,
the bad tree
had grown back,
had sprung up
new and bigger,
and more beautiful
and ugly.

It was very discouraging.
They talked a lot about it,
and cut it down again,

and poured gasoline on the roots,
and burned all the leaves and branches
in a big fire.
After the smoldering embers
got cold,
the tree grew back,
bigger,
more bad,
and really gorgeous.

Other people
had been watching
from their houses,
waiting their turn.
They thought themselves
smarter,
with higher intellectual
capabilities,
they knew how
to get rid of the tree.
It was a growing plant,
a wood tree
that grew in the earth.

They incinerated it,
burned the roots
with chemicals,
vaporizing acids,
and robotic lasers,
detonated
on the ground,
bombed
from the air,
hit
with smart missiles,

and bombarded
with radiation.
They made
a fire storm;
and covered the ground
with concrete
and steel.

The tree grew back,
more fresh,
more elegant, even gracious;
and really ugly.
The wood was
harder,
darker,
more shiny,
thick hot muscle,
and the leaves,
full and lush,
moved like underwater plants
luxuriously in the breeze.

Everyone was extremely discouraged,
extremely depressed,
a catastrophe.
They had made for themselves
a hell world.

They talked incessantly about it,
and came to a big decision.
The Mayor resigned
in disgrace,
and those, who had worked
so hard,
left,

humiliated,
departed,
moved to the other side of town,
stayed away.

Then, out of the blue, appeared
these beautiful people,
They were simple
and humble,
and a little like peacocks,
and seemingly well-intentioned,
with a great sense of humor.
Radiantly relaxed,
oozing
loving kindness
and compassion,
they walked right up,
and started eating
the leaves.
They ate the leaves
and enjoyed them,
became happy,
and laughed
and laughed;
and chomped on more leaves.
You could tell they really
liked the taste.

They pressed
their cheeks
to the flowers,
black velvet
coated with transmission oil.
They licked
the sweet juices

that seeped
from the petals.
The pollen
was coal dust
and petroleum gas.
Burying their noses,
they sucked
in deep breaths,
eating
the smell,
great bliss.

They discovered the fruit
hidden beneath the leaves,
overripe mangoes
with sticky eggplant skin,
hung like testicles;
and inside the fruit
was rotting meat,
like liver.
The special people
got their faces
into the stinking slime,
and really got into it;
inhaling with their lips,
and teeth,
and tongues.
They licked and drank
the thick red juice.
The seeds,
like cabochon rubies,
seemed particularly potent,
and were chewed
with great delight.

The fruit contained
the five wisdoms.
The men and women
became luminous,
their skin was golden
and their bodies,
almost transparent,
were clothed in shimmering
rainbow lights.

They became sleepy,
yawned, and curled up
under the tree,
and a took a nap.
While they slept,
music filled the air.
Lounging
against the gnarled tree trunk
and protruding roots,
their huge bodies
colored red, yellow,
blue, green, white,
rested in
great equanimity,
and radiated
huge compassion.

Inside the tree
were the secret homes
of many demi-gods,
hungry ghosts,
and earth spirits,
who were very pleased
with all the positive attention
being paid them.

After years of abuse
mutilation
and destruction,
they were thrilled;
even though they were being ravaged
and their flowers wrecked.

At the root endings,
there were jewels,
diamonds and emeralds and rubies,
which were stars in the sky
of the world below.

The beautiful men and women
woke up,
and nibbled on the leaves again.
They ate the leaves,
like deer,
pausing between bites,
looking up
at the vast
empty sky.
The leaves and fruit
increased their clarity
and bliss,
and introduced the nature
of primordially pure
wisdom mind.

(2001)

LA SAGGEZZA DELLE STREGHE (WISDOM OF THE WITCHES)

On a cold, early November night,
Mimmo, Martino, and I climbed to the top
of the Norman rock tower of Castelmezzano.
In the green lips of the trees,
the Dolomite mountain peaks of Basilicata,
big, broken, splintered teeth spiked into the sky,
and a thin crescent moon.
Fog blew in from the blackness,
clouds rolled in below
and swirled around us,
and exposed briefly by a beam of light,
fled quickly, slipped back into the pitch black,
stumbled up and danced down the stone slopes,
and rushed in to touch, embrace and welcome us.

Hidden inside the fog and mists
were witches,
each a secret to herself,
the white witch with the curved knife and the bella figura,
the red witch made of ruby with a voluptuous body,
the blue witch with an owl face
rode a donkey with three legs,
the yellow witch wore a ball gown of gold brocade
and held a mongoose vomiting jewels,
the green witch with a hawk face rode a camel
and scorpions came from her fingertips,
and the beautiful witch with a smiling face
held a lamp of the sun and moon,
the witches of fog ate the witches of snow,
and witches dressed in black rode white dogs,
and danced, flew, chased, glided, and leaped over,

and long dives from life to death,
and witches who were rotting in hell
swarmed, screeching with joy.
They were happy to see us.

The witch Santa Meurte was a skeleton
with a grim-reaper sickle and a blood curdling grin.
She usually wore black,
but occasionally liked feather boas and sequin gowns,
and big fake jewels and necklaces,
and rings on each bone finger.
She chain smoked cigarettes and joints,
drank whiskey straight, and snorted drugs.
She had no flesh, but loved sex and bliss.
She danced exquisitely the criminal tango.
Santa Meurte answered the prayers of the poorest
and most outcast,
people in trouble adored her,
whores and drug dealers,
car thieves, burglars, and con-artists sought her protection,
people prayed for the miracle of money for food,
and the lost and abandoned.
Every single one who asked her help, she helped.
Santa Meurte was the wish-fulfilling witch.

The witch of poetry was Sarasvati
and her sister Laxmi was the witch of wealth.
When Sarasvati wrote great poems
and sang beautiful songs
and filled the world with music and wisdom,
and became famous and adored
for her brilliance, beauty, and compassion,
her sister Laxmi got very jealous, and angry,
and did the most terrible things.
She stole the cash and property,

lied, invented false gossip,
had her excluded,
and had the lawyers sue
blocking everything from happening;
she punished her for her success,
sweet revenge.
That is why poets never have money.
Poets are poor sisters,
with great clarity and great bliss.

Put your ear to stone
and open your heart to the sky,
put your ear to stone
and open your heart to the sky,
put your ear to stone
and open your heart to the sky,
put your ear to stone
and open your heart to the sky.

Ugly and beautiful witches,
peaceful and wrathful witches,
increasing and magnanimous witches,
are the outer displays of wisdom,
witches of water, witches of earth,
witches of fire, witches of air,
witches of space
are the inner wisdoms,
witches of fabulous sex in the union of great bliss
are the secret wisdoms,
and witches of great compassion and emptiness
are the innermost wisdoms.

Mimmo, Martino, and I climbed back down
the rocky mountain path,
as if feathers were under our feet,
and we walked down below the clouds,
on steps cut in the rock toward the medieval stone houses
that clung to the edge of the mountain peaks,
thousands of modulating waves of sweet sound
sang in silence.

(2003)

DEMONS IN THE DETAILS

For William Burroughs, Allen Ginsberg, Brion Gysin and some others

Once upon a time,
these friends
loved
each other
very much,
and they made a vow
to stay together
until they all
attained
Enlightenment,

and lifetime
after lifetime,
and endless
re-births,
and doing practice,
they all realized
the absolute
empty
true nature
of mind.

They were so
happy
and overjoyed,
they started
dancing,
and dancing,
and danced
and danced,

they were so happy,
in the shocked
recognition
of emptiness
and compassion,
they kept
on dancing,
and dancing
and dancing
and dancing,
and they danced away
all their flesh
and skin,
until there was
nothing
left
but their bones,
and they kept dancing
in their bones,
dancing
skeletons
dancing skeletons.

Smooth
skulls
and speeding
smiling
teeth
and wide eyed
holes,
sliding
femurs
and cracking
shins,
spinning

and sparkling
spinning and sparkling
spinal chords,
shouting
ribs
and singing
jaws,
squirming
pelvises,
shivering
bones
and shaking
bones;

I want to
jump
into your heart,
I'm gonna come
in your heart
from here.

When it gets too hot
for comfort
and you can't get
ice cream cones,
taint
no sin,
to take off
your skin
and dance around
in your bones
taint no sin,
to take off your skin
and dance around
in your bones.

You generated
enough
compassion
to fill the world,
and now,
resting in
great equanimity,
you have accomplished
great clarity
and great bliss,
and the vast
empty
expanse
of primordially pure
Wisdom Mind.

But our friends
were not
totally,
not completely
Enlightened
beings;
and sometimes
a hundred thousand years
in one of the
fabulous
god worlds
or highest
heavens,
is one year
or a couple of years
here in ours,
so much for that.

Now,
at this very moment,
each of their consciousnesses
is terrorized,
the bells
of hell
the bells of hell
the bells of hell
the bells of hell,
they have
cut off
your head,
and are shitting
down
your throat,
the worst
is at this moment
happening,
the very worst
is happening
now,
life
goes on.

(2000)

WELCOMING THE FLOWERS

I am standing on the corner of Stanton and Chrystie,
waiting for the traffic light to change.
A man is sitting on the steps of a building
holding his young son on his lap.
He is eating fried chicken
from Chico's take-out on Houston.
He chews on the wings
and feeds bits of the breast to his son.

The man finishes eating
and puts the leftover chicken and bones,
fries and soda can in a paper bag
and leaves it on the sidewalk.
A brown dog from a neighboring building,
snoops around
gets his nose in the bag,
chews on the bones
and makes a mess.
The man hits the dog with a newspaper,
and it yelps and runs away.
A black cat sitting in a window,
watches wide-eyed,
staring down at the dog,
chicken bones and gristle.

I see their past and present lives.
The man eats the chicken
and the chicken
was his mother,
who had died of cancer two years ago;
the dog chewing on the bones
was his father,

who had died of a heart attack five years ago;
and the cat in the window
was his grandmother;
and his young son, whom he holds so tenderly,
was the man who killed him in his previous life.
His wife comes home with groceries
and takes the boy into the building.
She had been his lover in many past lives,
and was his mother for the first time in this one.
The world just makes me laugh.

Fill what is empty,
empty what is full,
light
as body,
light
as breath.

Welcoming the flowers:
daffodils
baptized in butter,
lilacs lasciviously licking the air,
necklaces of wisteria
bowing to magnolia mamas,
the cherry blossoms are razor blades,
the snow dahlias are sharp as cat piss,
the lilies of the valley are
lilies of fur,
lilies of feather,
lilies of fin,
lilies of skin,
the almost Miss America rose,
and they all smell so good
and I am sucked into their meaty earthy goodness.

You make
my heart
feel warm,
I lay my head on your chest
and feel free,
filling
what is empty,
emptying
what is full,
filling what is
empty, emptying
what is full,
filling what is empty, emptying what is full,
filling what is empty, emptying what is full,
the gods
we know
we are,
the gods
we knew
we were.

I smell you
with my eyes,
see you
with my ears,
feel you
with my lips,
taste you
with my nose,
hear you
with my tongue,
I want you to sit
in my heart,
and smile.

Words come from sound,
sound comes from wisdom,
wisdom comes from emptiness,
deep relaxation
of great perfection.

Welcoming the flowers:
armfuls of honey suckle
and columbine,
red-tipped knives of Indian paint brush,
the fields of daisies are the people
who betrayed me
the lupine were self-serving and unkind,
orchids are the tongues that lied,
hyacinths are the songs of suicides,
the voluminous and voluptuous bougainvillea
are licking fire loving what cannot burn,
the big bunch of one thousand red roses
are all the people I made love to,
hit my nose with stem of a rose,
the poppies have pockets packed with narcotic treats,
the chrysanthemums are a garland of skulls.

I go to death
willingly,
with the same comfort and bliss
as when I lay my head
on my lover's chest.

Welcoming the flowers,
the third bouquet is a crown of blue bells,
a carillon of foxglove,
a sunflower snuggles its head on my lap
and gazes up at the sky,

may all the tiny black insects
crawling on the peony petals
be my sons and daughters in future lives,
great balls of light
white, red, blue
concentric dazzle,
yellow, green
great exaltation,
the world just makes me laugh.

May sound and light
not rise up and appear as enemies,
may I know all sound as my own sound,
may I know all light as my own light,
may I spontaneously know all phenomena as myself,
may I realize original nature,
not fabricated by mind,
empty
naked awareness.

(2004)

THANX 4 NOTHING

On My 70th Birthday In 2006

I want to give my thanks to everyone for everything,
and as a token of my appreciation,
I want to offer back to you all my good and bad habits
as magnificent priceless jewels,
wish-fulfilling gems satisfying everything you need and want,
thank you, thank you, thank you,
thanks.

May every drug I ever took
come back and get you high,
may every glass of vodka and wine I ever drank
come back and make you feel really good,
numbing your nerve ends
allowing the natural clarity of your mind to flow free,
may all the suicides be songs of aspiration,
thanks that bad news is always true,
may all the chocolate I've ever eaten
come back rushing through your bloodstream
and make you feel happy,
thanks for allowing me to be a poet
a noble effort, doomed, but the only choice.

I want to thank you for your kindness and praise,
thanks for celebrating me,
thanks for the resounding applause,
I want to thank you for taking everything for yourself
and giving nothing back,
you were always only self-serving,
thanks for exploiting my big ego
and making me a star for your own benefit,
thanks that you never paid me,

thanks for all the sleaze,
thanks for being mean and rude
and smiling at my face,
I am happy that you robbed me,
I am happy that you lied
I am happy that you helped me,
thanks, grazie, merci beaucoup.

May you smoke a joint with William,
and spend intimate time with his mind,
more profound than any book he wrote,
I give enormous thanks to all my lovers,
beautiful men with brilliant minds,
great artists,
Bob, Jasper, Ugo,
may they come here now
and make love to you,
and may my many other lovers
of totally great sex,
countless
lovers
of boundless
fabulous sex
countless lovers
of boundless fabulous sex
countless lovers of boundless fabulous sex
countless lovers of boundless
fabulous sex
in the golden age of promiscuity,
may they all come here now,
and make love to you,
if you want,
may they hold you in their arms
balling
to your hearts

delight.
balling to your hearts
delight
balling to
your hearts delight
balling to your hearts delight.

May all the people who are dead
Allen, Brion, Lita, Jack,
and I do not miss any of you
I don't miss any of them,
no nostalgia,
it was wonderful that we loved each other
but I do not want any of them back;
now, if any of you
are attracted to any of them,
may they come back from the dead,
and do whatever is your pleasure,
may they multiply,
and be the slaves
of whomever wants them,
fulfilling your every wish and desire,
(but you won't want them as masters,
as they're demons),
may Andy come here
fall in love with you
and make each of you a superstar,
everyone can have
Andy.
everyone can
have Andy.
everyone can have Andy,
everyone can have an Andy.

Huge hugs to the friends who betrayed me,
every friend became an enemy,
sooner or later,
big kisses to my loves that failed,
I am delighted you are vacuum cleaners
sucking everything into your dirt bags,
you are none other than a reflection of my mind.

Thanks for the depression problem
and feeling like suicide
everyday of my life,
and now that I'm seventy,
I am happily almost there.

Twenty billion years ago,
in the primordial wisdom soup
beyond comprehension and indescribable,
something without substance moved slightly,
and became something imperceptible,
moved again and became something invisible,
moved again and produced a particle and particles,
moved again and became a quark,
again and became quarks,
moved again and again and became protons and neutrons,
and the twelve dimensions of space,
tiny fire balls of primordial energy,
bits of energy tossed back and forth
in a game of catch between particles,
transmitting electromagnetic light
and going fast, 40 million times a second,
where the pebble hits the water,
that is where the trouble began,
something without substance became something with substance,
why did it happen?
because something substanceless
had a feeling of missing out on something,

not getting it,
was not getting it
not getting it
not
getting it,
imperceptibly not having something
when there was nothing to have,
clinging to a notion of reality;
from the primordially endless potential,
to modern reality,
twenty billion years later,
has produced me and my stupid grasping mind,
has made me and you, and my grasping mind.

May Rinpoche and all the great Tibetan teachers who loved me,
come back and love you more,
may they hold you in their wisdom hearts,
bathe you in all-pervasive compassion,
give you pith instructions,
and may you with the diligence of Olympic athletes
do meditation practice,
and may you with direct confidence
realize the true nature of mind.

America, thanks for the neglect,
I did it without you,
let us celebrate poetic justice,
you and I never were,
never tried to do anything,
and never succeeded,
thanks for introducing me
to the face of the naked mind,
thanx 4 nothing.

(2007)

ACKNOWLEDGMENTS

The editor would like to thank Stephen Voyce and Suzanne Zelazo for transcribing and proofreading many of these poems. He also gratefully acknowledges the support of a Standard Grant from the Social Sciences and Humanities Research Council of Canada for work on this book.

Printed in the United States
by Baker & Taylor Publisher Services